CliffsNo

Shakespeare's
The Tempest

By Sheri Metzger, Ph.D.

IN THIS BOOK

- Learn about the Life and Background of the Author
- Preview an Introduction to the Play
- Study a graphical Character Map
- Explore themes and literary devices in the Critical Commentaries
- Examine in-depth Character Analyses
- Enhance your understanding of the work with Critical Essays
- Reinforce what you learn with CliffsNotes Review
- Find additional information to further your study in CliffsNotes Resource Center and online at www.cliffsnotes.com

IDG Books Worldwide, Inc.
An International Data Group Company
Foster City, CA • Chicago, IL • Indianapolis, IN • New York, NY

About the Author

Sheri Metzger currently teaches literature and composition in the University Honors Program and in the English Department at the University of New Mexico, where she has taught for the past ten years.

Publisher's Acknowledgments

Editorial

Project Editor: Tracy Barr

Acquisitions Editor: Greg Tubach

Glossary Editors: The editors and staff at Webster's New World™ Dictionaries

Editorial Administrator: Michelle Hacker

Production

Indexer: York Production Services, Inc.

Proofreader: York Production Services, Inc.

IDG Books Indianapolis Production Department

CliffsNotes™ Shakespeare's *The Tempest*

Published by

IDG Books Worldwide, Inc.

An International Data Group Company

919 E. Hillsdale Blvd.

Suite 300

Foster City, CA 94404

www.idgbooks.com (IDG Books Worldwide Web site)

www.cliffsnotes.com (CliffsNotes Web site)

Copyright © 2001 IDG Books Worldwide, Inc. All rights reserved. No part of this book, including interior design, cover design, and icons, may be reproduced or transmitted in any form, by any means (electronic, photocopying, recording, or otherwise) without the prior written permission of the publisher.

Library of Congress Control Number: 00-107705

ISBN: 0-7645-8674-2

Printed in the United States of America

10 9 8 7 6 5 4 3 2 1

1B/SX/RR/QQ/IN

Distributed in the United States by IDG Books Worldwide, Inc.

Distributed by CDG Books Canada Inc. for Canada; by Transworld Publishers Limited in the United Kingdom; by IDG Norge Books for Norway; by IDG Sweden Books for Sweden; by IDG Books Australia Publishing Corporation Pty. Ltd. for Australia and New Zealand; by TransQuest Publishers Pte Ltd. for Singapore, Malaysia, Thailand, Indonesia, and Hong Kong; by Gotop Information Inc. for Taiwan; by ICG Muse, Inc. for Japan; by Norma Comunicaciones S.A. for Columbia; by Intersoft for South Africa; by Eyrolles for France; by International Thomson Publishing for Germany, Austria and Switzerland; by Distribuidora Cuspide for Argentina; by LR International for Brazil; by Galileo Libros for Chile; by Ediciones ZETA S.C.R. Ltda. for Peru; by WS Computer Publishing Corporation, Inc., for the Philippines; by Contemporanea de Ediciones for Venezuela; by Express Computer Distributors for the Caribbean and West Indies; by Micronesia Media Distributor, Inc. for Micronesia; by Grupo Editorial Norma S.A. for Guatemala; by Chips Computadoras S.A. de C.V. for Mexico; by Editorial Norma de Panama S.A. for Panama; by American Bookshops for Finland. Authorized Sales Agent: Anthony Rudkin Associates for the Middle East and North Africa.

For general information on IDG Books Worldwide's books in the U.S., please call our Consumer Customer Service department at **800-762-2974**.

For reseller information, including discounts and premium sales, please call our Reseller Customer Service department at **800-434-3422**.

For information on where to purchase IDG Books Worldwide's books outside the U.S., please contact our International Sales department at **317-572-3993** or fax **317-572-4002**.

For consumer information on foreign language translations, please contact our Customer Service department at **1-800-434-3422**, fax 317-572-4002, or e-mail rights@idgbooks.com.

For information on licensing foreign or domestic rights, please phone **+1-650-653-7098**.

For sales inquiries and special prices for bulk quantities, please contact our Order Services department at **800-434-3422** or write to the address above.

For information on using IDG Books Worldwide's books in the classroom or for ordering examination copies, please contact our Educational Sales department at **800-434-2086** or fax **317-572-4005**.

For press review copies, author interviews, or other publicity information, please contact our Public Relations department at **650-653-7000** or fax **650-653-7500**.

For authorization to photocopy items for corporate, personal, or educational use, please contact Copyright Clearance Center, 222 Rosewood Drive, Danvers, MA 01923, or fax **978-750-4470**.

 is a registered trademark under exclusive license to IDG Books Worldwide, Inc. from International Data Group, Inc.

Table of Contents

How to Use This Book

CliffsNotes Shakespeare's *The Tempest* supplements the original work, giving you background information about the author, an introduction to the novel, a graphical character map, critical commentaries, expanded glossaries, and a comprehensive index. CliffsNotes Review tests your comprehension of the original text and reinforces learning with questions and answers, practice projects, and more. For further information on Shakespeare and *The Tempest*, check out the CliffsNotes Resource Center.

CliffsNotes provides the following icons to highlight essential elements of particular interest:

 Reveals the underlying themes in the work.

 Helps you more easily relate to or discover the depth of a character.

 Uncovers elements such as setting, atmosphere, mystery, passion, violence, irony, symbolism, tragedy, foreshadowing, and satire.

 Enables you to appreciate the nuances of words and phrases.

Don't Miss Our Web Site

Discover classic literature as well as modern-day treasures by visiting the Cliffs-Notes Web site at www.cliffsnotes.com. You can obtain a quick download of a CliffsNotes title, purchase a title in print form, browse our catalog, or view online samples.

You'll also find interactive tools that are fun and informative, links to interesting Web sites, tips, articles, and additional resources to help you, not only for literature, but for test prep, finance, careers, computers, and the Internet too. See you at www.cliffsnotes.com!

LIFE AND BACKGROUND OF THE AUTHOR

Shakespeare's Early Life

Only a few documents chronicle William Shakespeare's life, and thus scholars have been forced to attempt a reconstruction of the playwright's life based on whatever official documents have survived. Shakespeare's father moved to Stratford-upon-Avon, from nearby Snitterfield, sometime before 1557, when he married Mary Arden, the daughter of a prosperous farmer. John Shakespeare was a leather worker and merchant who held several posts in local government after he settled in Stratford.

After the couple married, they had eight children. William Shakespeare was the third child and the first son born to the couple. His baptism was recorded April 26, 1564, and although the exact date of his birth is not known, it is now celebrated on April 23, which is also the day on which he died, 52 years later.

Education and Marriage

Shakespeare's education is a matter of speculation because no school records have ever been found, but it is likely that he attended the local grammar school, King's New School, which emphasized a liberal arts education. Shakespeare would have learned Latin while at this school, since the study of Latin was central to most Elizabethan education. His education ended after grammar school, and Shakespeare did not attend university.

In November 1582, an 18-year-old Shakespeare married 26-year-old Anne Hathaway. Their daughter Susanna was baptized six months later. On February 2, 1585, twins, Hamnet and Judith, were also baptized. Hamnet died at age 11, but both Susanna and Judith lived to be adults, marrying, and providing Shakespeare with grandchildren.

There are no definitive records of Shakespeare's life between the birth of his twins in 1585 and reference to his stage success, noted in a letter dated 1592, but it is thought that he went to London sometime around 1587 or 1588. Records indicate that Shakespeare appeared as an actor and as a playwright. He also made money as shareholder in an acting company, The Lord Chamberlain's Men, and as such, he would have received a share of the gate receipts. But most actors and playwrights depended on patronage for their survival, and this was also true for Shakespeare. Eventually, Shakespeare became one of the owners of the Globe Theatre, which was built in 1599. He later also became an investor in the Blackfriars Theatre, which opened in 1609. Shakespeare wrote many of his plays specifically for performance in these two theatres.

Literary Works

Shakespeare was very casual about the publication of his works, apparently having little interest in saving his writings. The 1623 Folio contains most of Shakespeare's plays, but they were not published in chronological order and do not include the dates of their original composition. Instead, the best scholars can do is examine the quarto editions, published during Shakespeare's life, or references from contemporary letters or diaries and try to determine from those dates the possible timeframe for a play's first performance.

After careful research, scholars have assigned probable dates of composition to Shakespeare's work, and those dates, used by the editors of the *Oxford Shakespeare* and adopted by other editors, including the editors of the *Norton Shakespeare*, will be used in the following discussion of the texts' probable dates of composition. In general, the plays before 1600 were histories and romantic comedies. After 1600, tragedies became the focus of Shakespeare's work, while the problem comedies, such as *The Tempest*, were darker in content, exploring serious social and moral problems.

Plays before 1600

Two Gentlemen of Verona is thought to be the first play written by Shakespeare. It was first published in the 1623 Folio but thought to have been composed in 1590–91.

The Taming of the Shrew may have been written in 1592 or earlier, but it was also first published in the 1623 Folio.

The Tragedy of King Richard the Third, with a first printing in 1597, was probably first performed in 1592–93.

The First Part of the Contention of the Two Famous Houses of York and Lancaster (*The Second Part of Henry VI*) was probably composed about 1594.

The Comedy of Errors, although not published until 1623, was presumably written much earlier and was first performed in 1594.

Titus Andronicus, the first of Shakespeare's Latin plays, the revenge tragedy, was printed in 1594.

The First Part of Henry the Sixth is often attributed to multiple authors, and there are no printed editions prior to the 1623 Folio, but the play is thought to have been performed for the first time in 1594–95.

Richard Duke of York (*3 Henry VI*) was first printed in 1595.

Love's Labour's Lost followed in 1594–95 and was followed by *Love's Labour's Won*, which survives only in a small fragment.

A Midsummer Night's Dream may have been performed as early as 1595, although it was not printed until 1600. *The Most Excellent and Lamentable Tragedy of Romeo and Juliet*, first published in 1597, is also thought to have been composed in 1595. Both plays offer contrasting views of love and marriage.

While it was not published until 1623, *The Life and Death of King John* is usually dated at about 1596.

The Tragedy of King Richard the Second followed, but this play, whose abdication scene was said to have been deleted during the lifetime of Elizabeth I, was not printed until 1597.

Because of its perceived anti-Semitic content, *The Merchant of Venice* has been surrounded in controversy, but when it was first registered in 1598, its content simply reflected accepted views.

Shakespeare turned once again to history for inspiration with the composition of *The History of Henry the Fourth* (*1 Henry IV*), first printed in 1598.

A comedy appeared next with the composition of *The Merry Wives of Windsor* in 1597–98.

Although not printed until 1600, Shakespeare probably wrote *The Second Part of Henry Fourth* immediately after he finished the first play in the sequence.

As he had done in the past, Shakespeare penned a comedy after the historical play, this time *Much Ado About Nothing*, probably composed in 1598.

The Life of Henry the Fifth soon followed in 1599.

Another history followed, but this time Shakespeare turned to early Roman history for inspiration. Although *The Tragedy of Julius Caesar* was not published until 1623, its composition is thought to be 1598–99.

With the composition of *As You Like It*, probably in 1599, Shakespeare recalls the influences of earlier pastoral poetry; however, this comedy marks the end of the playwright's light romantic comedies.

Plays after 1600

The year 1600 represents the beginning of a new phase in Shakespeare's compositions with the printing of *The Tragedy of Hamlet, Prince of Denmark*.

Twelfth Night, or What You Will followed a year later and marked a move toward darker comedies with complex plots and characters who are often cruel rather than comic.

With *Troilus and Cressida* in 1601–02, Shakespeare turns to Greek antiquity and the *Iliad* for inspiration, although as usual, Shakespeare rewrites the story to suit his needs.

Measure for Measure is another of Shakespeare's dark comedies, not published until 1623 but first performed in 1604.

During the same period (1603–04), Shakespeare was also writing *The Tragedy of Othello, the Moor of Venice*, and *All's Well that Ends Well*, a complex comedy that raises questions about accepted gender roles.

With *The Life of Timons of Athens*, Shakespeare again turns to history, but this play, as with several others, was first published in the 1623 Folio.

The History of King Lear or *The Tragedy of King Lear*, first printed in 1607–08, exists in two different texts, which are often published on facing pages or combined into one text.

The composition of *The Tragedy of Macbeth* followed and is usually dated at 1606. At the same time, Shakespeare was writing his sequel to *Julius Caesar, The Tragedy of Antony and Cleopatra*.

Pericles, Prince of Tyre, probably 1607–08, is thought to be a collaboration between Shakespeare and George Wilkins.

With *Coriolanus* in 1608, Shakespeare again finds his source in Roman history.

After 1610, Shakespeare left London and returned to Stratford and semi-retirement. But he continued to write plays, with *The Winter's Tale* (1609–11), *Cymbeline, King of Britain* (1609–10), and *The Tempest* (1611) largely composed in Stratford.

Shakespeare's life as a playwright concluded with his creation of *All Is True* or, as it was also known, *The Famous History of the Life of Henry the Eighth* (1613) and *The Two Noble Kinsmen* (1613–14).

His Other Works

Shakespeare's genius was not confined to the many plays he wrote and produced. He also wrote poetry. The long narrative poem *Venus and Adonis* was published in 1593, the first of Shakespeare's works to actually be published by Shakespeare. This poem was followed by another long narrative poem—*The Rape of Lucrece*, first published in 1594.

While writing his plays, Shakespeare was also composing sonnets, a format adapted by English poets from its Petrarchan origins. Although he probably began composing sonnets early in his writing career, evidence exists that Shakespeare continued revising his sonnets during the 1590s and through the early 1600s, finally publishing the entire sequence in 1609. The sonnet sequence was followed by "A Lover's Complaint," which was probably composed earlier (1602—5), and a collection of occasional poems.

Shakespeare died April 23, 1616. Although Shakespeare's authorship of these plays has been questioned by those who suggest that he did not pen the works, he was quite well known in Elizabethan London, and it would have been difficult for a sustained conspiracy to exist. In the end, it really does not matter whether the man we know as William Shakespeare composed the plays attributed to him or not. The plays exist for our enjoyment, and that is sufficient.

INTRODUCTION TO THE PLAY

Introduction

Records indicate that *The Tempest* was performed before James I on November 1, 1611, but there may also have been earlier performances. *The Tempest* was again performed during the winter of 1612–13 to celebrate the marriage of Princess Elizabeth, the daughter of King James I. But this play was not printed until it appeared for the first time in the 1623 Folio.

It is relatively easy to date *The Tempest*'s composition, since Shakespeare used material that was not available until late 1610: letters from the new Virginia colony in Jamestown and an account of a 1609 shipwreck off Bermuda. Unlike many of Shakespeare's other plays, *The Tempest*, is not drawn from another, earlier literary work. There is no formal source, except for the ideas that the author might have found in reading accounts of the Bermuda shipwreck or the stories emerging from the new colonies, which had been recently established in the New World.

The Play as a Romance

The Tempest is a difficult play to categorize. Although it ends in a wedding and thus might be defined as a comedy, there are many serious undertones that diminish the comedic tone. Instead, most modern anthologies of Shakespeare's works list this play as a romance. This separate division of romances includes what are generally labeled as "the problem plays." Along with *The Tempest*, the romances include *Pericles*, *Cymbeline*, *The Winter's Tale*, and *The Two Noble Kinsmen*, plays of Shakespeare's later years. These plays were written between 1604 and 1614, just prior to his retirement, when Shakespeare was composing plays that combined romance with some of the darker aspects of life. The romances are plays with the potential for tragedy but in which these tragic elements are resolved.

With *The Tempest*, Shakespeare turns to fantasy and magic as a way to explore romantic love, sibling hatred, and the love of a father for his child. In addition, *The Tempest* examines many of the topics that Shakespeare had focused on in his earlier plays, topics such as the attempts to overthrow a king (*Macbeth*, *Richard II*, and *Julius Caesar*), nature versus nurture (*The Winter's Tale* and *King Lear*), and innocence (*Twelfth Night*).

Although *The Tempest* provides the first masque within a play, the idea of a play within a play had occurred in earlier works, such as *Hamlet* and *Much Ado About Nothing*. In many ways *The Tempest* serves as a culmination of Shakespeare's earlier work, since in this play, he brings many of these earlier ideas together in one work.

Historical and Cultural Context

By the beginning of the seventeenth century, the threat of the Black Death (the plague) was diminishing, but it still continued to be a seasonal problem in London, which was overcrowded and suffered from poor sanitation and too much poverty.

A hundred years earlier, Henry VII had formed alliances with neighboring countries and trade was flourishing in London. But the coming of trade changed the face of England. Instead of a country composed largely of an agrarian culture, England, and especially London, became an important center of trade. There was more wealth, and the newly rich could now afford to escape the congestion of the city. There was a need for large country estates, and so more and more farm land was enclosed.

Displaced rural families fled to the larger cities, where crowding, unemployment, and disease increased with the increase in population. As city life flourished, there was a resulting nostalgia for the loss of country life. In response to this sentimentality, England's poets began to compose poetry recalling the tranquility of rustic life.

Early in the seventeenth century, the masque that comprises much of the fourth act of *The Tempest* was becoming a regular form of court entertainment. Masques were elaborate spectacles, designed to appeal to the audience's senses and glorify the monarch. Furthermore, their sheer richness suggested the magnificence of the king's court; thus they served a political purpose as well as entertained.

It is important to remember that the masque fulfilled another important function, the desire to recapture the past. As is the case with most masques, Prospero's masque is focused on pastoral motifs, with reapers and nymphs celebrating the fecundity of the land.

The masques, with their pastoral themes, also responded to this yearning for a time now ended. The country life, with its abundance of harvests and peaceful existence, is an idealized world that ignores the realities of an agrarian life, with its many hardships. The harshness of winter and the loss of crops and animals are forgotten in the longing for the past.

Elaborate scenery, music, and costumes were essential elements of earlier masques, but during the Jacobean period, the masque became more ornate and much more expensive to stage. Eventually the cost became so great—and the tax burden on the poor so significant—that the masques became an important contributing cause for the English Revolution, and ultimately, the execution of Charles I.

Structure

There is really very little plot in *The Tempest*. There is the love story, and then there is story of two younger brothers who covet their older brothers' titles and possessions. And finally, there is the story of Caliban's plot to murder Prospero. But none of these plots are given much attention or substance; instead, the play is about the complexities of human nature and about reminding the audience that the division between happiness and tragedy is always fragile and must be carefully maintained.

Although *The Tempest* ends with the promise of a wedding, it could just as easily have ended with tragedy. In this play, there are two murder plots and a betrayal to resolve. In a tragedy, these might have ended with the stage awash in blood, as in *Hamlet*, but in *The Tempest*, Prospero's careful manipulation of all the characters and their plans also controls the direction of the action. Prospero's avoidance of tragedy reveals his character's decency and contradicts some critics' arguments that he is an amoral demigod exploiting the natural inhabitants of this island.

The Tempest is unique in its adherence to the three unities. In his *Poetics*, Aristotle argued that *unity of action* was essential for dramatic structure. This meant that a dramatic work should have a clear beginning, middle, and end. The *unity of time* is derived from Aristotle's argument that all the action should occur within one revolution of the sun—one day. The *unity of place* developed later and is a Renaissance idea, which held that the location of the play should be limited to one place. These unities added verisimilitude to the work and made it easier for the audience to believe the events unfolding on stage.

Shakespeare rarely used the three unities, but he uses them in this play, something he has only done in one other play, *The Comedy of Errors*. All the events occur on the island and within one brief three-hour period. Shakespeare needed the three unities, especially that of time, to counter the incredulity of the magic and to add coherence to the plot.

The Tempest, although it is one of Shakespeare's shortest plays, still maintains the integrity of the five-act structure. In fact, most Elizabethan theatre adheres to the five-act structure, which corresponds to divisions in the action. The first act is the Exposition, in which the playwright sets forth the problem and introduces the main characters. In *The Tempest*, the first act establishes the nature of Antonio's betrayal of Prospero, and it explains how Prospero and Miranda came to live on the island. This first act also opens with a violent storm, which establishes the extent of Prospero's power. Most of the play's remaining characters also make an appearance in this act.

The second act is the Complication, in which the entanglement or conflict is developed. In *The Tempest*, the conspiracy to murder Alonso is developed, which establishes that Antonio is still an unsavory character. In addition, the audience learns more about Caliban, and Stefano and Trinculo appear, allowing the groundwork for a second conspiracy to be formed.

The third act is the Climax; and as the name suggests, this is when the action takes a turning point and the crisis occurs. In a romance, this is the point at which the young lovers assert their love, although there may be complications. It is important that the way to love not be too easy, and so in *The Tempest*, Prospero has forbidden contact between Miranda and Ferdinand, although the audience knows this is only a pretense. In this act, the conspiracy to murder Prospero is developed, although the audience knows that Ariel is listening, and so there is no real danger. And finally, the essential climactic moment occurs in this act when Prospero confronts his enemies at the ghostly banquet.

The fourth act is called the Falling Action, which signals the beginning of the play's resolution. In this act, the romance between Ferdinand and Miranda is acknowledged and celebrated with a masque, and Prospero deals with the conspiracy to murder him by punishing Caliban, Stefano, and Trinculo.

The fifth act is called the Catastrophe, wherein the conclusion occurs. As the name suggests, this act brings closure to the play, a resolution to the conflict, and the plans for a wedding. As the play draws to a close, Prospero is victorious over his enemies, Ferdinand is reunited with his father, Antonio and Sebastian are vanquished, and Caliban regrets his plotting.

Literary Devices

Students of Shakespeare's plays quickly come to appreciate the literary devices that the playwright employs in constructing his plays. For example, most Shakespearean plays contain *soliloquies,* which offer a way for the playwright to divulge a character's inner thoughts. The soliloquy requires that the character must think that he is alone on stage, as he reveals to the audience what he is really thinking. In *The Tempest,* the soliloquy is not used as often as it would be in a tragedy, because the dramatic moments are not as intense. However, Prospero still uses this device, most notably in Act V, when he tells the audience what he has accomplished with the help of magic and that soon he will no longer have need for such devices.

A soliloquy is different from a *monologue*, in which a character speaks aloud his thoughts, but with other characters present. Shakespeare also frequently employs the *aside*, in which the character addresses the audience, but other characters do not hear these words. There is a suggestion of conspiracy in the aside, which allows the audience to learn details that most of the characters on stage do not know. For example, Miranda uses an aside in Act I, Scene 2, when she confides to the audience her concern for her father. The aside is usually assumed to be truthful.

Shakespeare's Language

Shakespeare's Elizabethan language can sometimes intimidate his audience. Shakespeare wrote most of *The Tempest* in verse, using iambic pentameter. *Iambic pentameter* is a literary term that defines the play's meter and the stresses placed on each syllable. In iambic pentameter, each complete line contains ten syllables, with each pair of syllables containing both an accented syllable and an unaccented syllable. Many

Renaissance poets used iambic pentameter because the alternating stresses create a rhythm that contributes to the beauty of the play's language.

Shakespeare also included prose passages in his plays, with prose lines being spoken by characters of lower social rank. Shakespeare uses this device to reveal the complexity of Caliban. In *The Tempest*, Caliban speaks prose when he is conspiring with Stefano and Trinculo, but when Caliban speaks of the beauty of the island, he speaks in verse.

Shakespeare's Elizabethan language can be difficult to understand at first. Use of a Shakespearean glossary and the *Oxford English Dictionary* are two sources that can help in understanding the language, but the biggest assist comes with practice. Reading and listening to Shakespeare's words becomes easier with practice. Reading aloud also helps in becoming familiar with early modern English. With time, the unfamiliar language and the rhetorical devices that Shakespeare employed in writing his texts cease to be strange, and the language assumes the beauty that is hidden within it.

Brief Synopsis

The Tempest opens in the midst of a storm, as a ship containing the king of Naples and his party struggles to stay afloat. On land, Prospero and his daughter, Miranda, watch the storm envelop the ship. Prospero has created the storm with magic, and he explains that his enemies are on board the ship.

The story Prospero relates is that he is the rightful Duke of Milan and that his younger brother, Antonio, betrayed him, seizing his title and property. Twelve years earlier, Prospero and Miranda were put out to sea in little more than a raft. Miraculously, they both survived and arrived safely on this island, where Prospero learned to control the magic that he now uses to manipulate everyone on the island. Upon his arrival, Prospero rescued a sprite, Ariel, who had been imprisoned by the witch Sycorax. Ariel wishes to be free and his freedom has been promised within two days. The last inhabitant of the island is the child of Sycorax and the devil: Caliban, whom Prospero has enslaved. Caliban is a natural man, uncivilized and wishing only to have his island returned to him to that he can live alone in peace.

Soon the royal party from the ship is cast ashore and separated into three groups. The king's son, Ferdinand, is brought to Prospero, where he sees Miranda, and the two fall instantly in love. Meanwhile, Alonso, the king of Naples, and the rest of his party have come ashore on another part of the island. Alonso fears that Ferdinand is dead and grieves for the loss of his son. Antonio, Prospero's younger brother, has also been washed ashore with the king's younger brother, Sebastian. Antonio easily convinces Sebastian that Sebastian should murder his brother and seize the throne for himself. This plot to murder Alonso is similar to Antonio's plot against his own brother, Prospero, 12 years earlier.

Another part of the royal party—the court jester and the butler—has also come ashore. Trinculo and Stefano each stumble upon Caliban, and each immediately sees a way to make money by exhibiting Caliban as a monster recovered from this uninhabited island. Stefano has come ashore in a wine cask, and soon Caliban, Trinculo, and Stefano are drunk. While drinking, Caliban hatches a plot to murder Prospero and enrolls his two new acquaintances as accomplices. Ariel is listening, however, and reports the plot to Prospero.

Meanwhile, Prospero has kept Ferdinand busy and has forbidden Miranda to speak to him, but the two still find time to meet and declare their love, which is actually what Prospero has planned. Next, Prospero stages a masque to celebrate the young couple's betrothal, with goddesses and nymphs entertaining the couple with singing and dancing.

While Ferdinand and Miranda have been celebrating their love, Alonso and the rest of the royal party have been searching for the king's son. Exhausted from the search and with the king despairing of ever seeing his son alive, Prospero has ghosts and an imaginary banquet brought before the king's party. A god-like voice accuses Antonio, Alonso, and Sebastian of their sins, and the banquet vanishes. The men are all frightened, and Alonso, Antonio, and Sebastian run away.

Prospero punishes Caliban, Trinculo, and Stefano with a run through a briar patch and swim in a scummy pond. Having accomplished what he set out to do, Prospero has the king's party brought in. Prospero is clothed as the rightful Duke of Milan, and when the spell has been removed, Alonso rejects all claims to Prospero's dukedom and apologizes for his mistakes. Within moments, Prospero reunites the king with his son, Ferdinand. Alonso is especially pleased to learn of Miranda's existence and that Ferdinand will marry her.

Prospero then turns to his brother, Antonio, who offers no regrets or apology for his perfidy. Nevertheless, Prospero promises not to punish Antonio as a traitor. When Caliban is brought in, Caliban tells Prospero that he has learned his lesson. His two co-conspirators, Trinculo and Stefano, will be punished by the king. Soon, the entire party retires to Prospero's cell to celebrate and await their departure home. Only Prospero is left on stage.

In a final speech, Prospero tells the audience that only with their applause will he be able to leave the island with the rest of the party. Prospero leaves the stage to the audience's applause.

List of Characters

Prospero   The rightful duke of Milan. After his brother, Antonio, seized his title and property, Prospero was exiled with his daughter and eventually found refuge on an island.

Miranda   Prospero's daughter. She has been on the island with her father for 12 years—since she was 3 years old.

Antonio   Prospero's younger brother, who is now the duke of Milan. He had plotted against Prospero years earlier and now convinces Sebastian to murder his brother, the king of Naples.

Ariel   A spirit of the air, he assists Prospero in seeking retribution over his enemies.

Caliban   The offspring of the witch Sycorax and the devil. Prospero has made Caliban his servant or slave, and in response, Caliban plots to murder Prospero.

Ferdinand   The son of the king of Naples. During the storm, he was separated from the rest of the king's party, met Miranda, and fell in love with her.

Alonso   The king of Naples. He believes his son has died and is overjoyed to later find him. Alonso is repentant for the pain he caused Prospero in the past.

Sebastian   Alonso's brother. He is easily led into planning his own brother's (the king's) murder.

Gonzalo   An elderly counselor who saves Prospero's and Miranda's lives when they are exiled. He provides a sense of hope and optimism when Ferdinand is lost.

Stefano   The king's butler. He arrives on the island drunk and quickly becomes involved in a plot to murder Prospero.

Trinculo   The king's jester. When Stefano arrives with wine, Trinculo joins him in drinking and then agrees to a plot to murder Prospero.

Francisco and Adrian   Two of the king's lords. They try to offer hope and protection to Alonso.

Boatswain   The ship's petty officer. He is in charge of the deck crew, the rigging, and the anchor. He must try to keep the boat afloat during the storm, even when the king's party makes demands upon his time.

Character Map

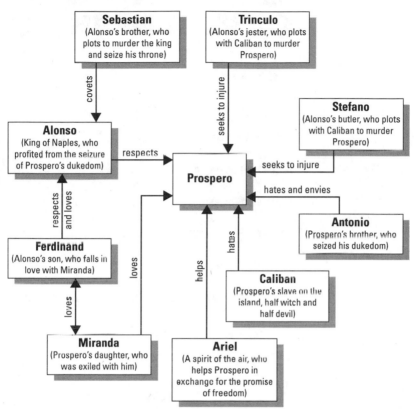

CRITICAL COMMENTARIES

Act I
Scene 1

Summary

    The Tempest opens in the midst of a fierce storm. The location is a ship at sea, with a royal party on board. As the sailors fight to save the ship, several of the royal passengers enter, and Alonso, the king, demands to know where the master (captain) is to be found. The boatswain, worried that the passengers will interfere, orders them to go below deck. The king's councilor, Gonzalo, reminds the boatswain that he is speaking to the king, but the boatswain points out that if the king really has so much power, he should use it to quell the storm. If he lacks this power, the royal party should go below decks, as the boatswain orders. The royal party exits, presumably to go below deck to seek shelter.

    Within moments, however, Antonio, Sebastian, and Gonzalo have returned topside again, much to the boatswain's annoyance. With Sebastian and Antonio cursing him, the boatswain continues in his efforts to save the ship. Soon, however, the sailors enter with laments that the ship is lost. Fearing that they will all soon die, Antonio, Sebastian, and Gonzalo elect to join the rest of the royal party below decks, where they will pray for their survival.

Commentary

Theme

    The opening confrontation between Gonzalo and the boatswain reveals one of the most important themes in *The Tempest*: class conflict, the discord between those who seize and hold power and those who are often the unwilling victims of power. When confronted by members of the royal party, the boatswain orders that they return below deck. He is performing his job, and to stop in response to Alonso's request for the master would be foolish. The boatswain cares little for Alonso's rank as king and asks, "What cares these roarers for the name of king?" (15–16). The king has no protection from the storm simply because of his rank, because the storm has little care for a man's social or political position. In response, Gonzalo urges the boatswain to remember that the king and his party are the passengers. The implication is that the boatswain should also remember that his social rank makes him subservient to the royal party, regardless of the circumstances. Gonzalo's words are a clear reminder that even in the midst of a storm, class or status remains an important part of life. However, the boatswain is not intimidated and responds that the royal party should "use your authority," to stop the storm (20–21). As far as the boatswain is concerned, all men are equal in a storm and all equally at risk.

Alonso seems to understand that the captain is the ship's final authority, at least initially. His original request for the master reflects his belief that the master is in charge of the ship, and that, as passengers, he (as king) and his retinue fall under the captain's authority. But alarm at the severity of the storm and frustration at the boatswain's order to go below decks causes the king's party to fall back on the rules of land—the king is the final authority. The boatswain's telling Gonzalo that the king should use his authority to stop the storm is a reminder that the king has no authority under these circumstances. Although he can control men (although not always with absolute certainty), even the king cannot control nature.

Literary Device

The storm and the subsequent rebellion on ship is a metaphor for the rebellion occurring in English society. In the Elizabethan and Jacobean world, English society was defined by its class system, in which individuals were born into specific classes by divine right. In the natural order of things (that is, the order defined by God), therefore, the aristocracy is superior. Although the characters of *The Tempest* are depicted as Italian in origin, their experiences and conflicts are English. Indeed, the passengers, who never forget that they are socially superior to the crew, need to be reminded that, during a storm, the captain of the ship is the final authority.

Furthermore, in the period just prior to the composition of *The Tempest*, English society had been rocked by political, social, and religious conflicts. The Gunpowder Plot (1605), for example, serves as an illustration of the conflict between the Protestant James and his Catholic subjects. The goal of the Roman Catholic conspirators was to murder James and kill the members of both houses of Parliament; fortunately for James, the plot failed. The social unrest in England, however, was exacerbated by James' extravagant spending on court entertainment, especially the lavishly staged masques, and the contrast between the poor and the rich became even more evident. Although James subjects lived in severe poverty, their burden was increased as they were taxed to pay for the king's masques. In response, unrest grew and would erupt several years later into revolution.

There are many tempests to be explored during the course of *The Tempest*. In addition to class conflict, there are also explorations into colonialism (English explorers had been colonizing the Americas) and a desire to find or create a utopian society. The storm scene that opens *The Tempest* establishes nature as an important element of the play and emphasizes the role of nature in society. Other tempests will be revealed in subsequent scenes, such as the emotional tempests that familial conflict creates (consider the conflict between Antonio and Prospero, and the coming conflict between Sebastian and Alonso); the tempests of discord (consider Caliban's dissatisfaction and desire for revenge) and of forbidden love (consider the romance between Miranda and Ferdinand). Finally, there are the tempests caused by the inherent conflict between generations. So, although *The Tempest* might correctly be called a romantic comedy, the title and the opening scene portend an exploration of conflicts more complex than romantic.

Glossary

(Here and in the following glossary sections, difficult words and phrases, as well as allusions and historical references, are explained.)

yarely briskly or smartly. Here the boatswain is instructing the sailors to move quickly or the ship will be pushed aground by the storm.

roarers noisy and unruly waves; here so called because they care little for royal rank.

boatswain the ship's petty officer, in charge of the deck crew, the rigging, anchors, boats, and so on.

drowning mark refers to a mole, located on the boatswain's face, the appearance of which was thought to portend a person's manner of death. In this case, the boatswain's mole appears to be the type that predicts a death by hanging.

merely [Obs.] absolutely; altogether; here, it means that they are completely cheated of their lives by drunkards.

Act I
Scene 2

Summary

Scene 2 opens on the island, with Prospero and Miranda watching the ship as it is tossed by the storm. Miranda knows that her father is creating the storm, and she begs him to end the ship's torment and her own, since she suffers as she watches the ship's inhabitants suffer. Prospero reassures his daughter that his actions have been to protect her. He also tells Miranda that she is ignorant of her heritage; he then explains the story of her birthright and of their lives before they came to be on the island.

Prospero begins his story with the news that he is the duke of Milan and Miranda is a princess. He also relates that he had abdicated day-to-day rule of his kingdom to his brother, Antonio. Prospero admits that books held more attraction than duties, and he willingly allowed his brother the opportunity to grasp control. But Antonio used his position to undermine Prospero and to plot against him. Prospero's trust in his brother proved unwise, when Antonio formed an alliance with the king of Naples to oust Prospero and seize his heritage. Prospero and his daughter were placed in a small, rickety boat and put out to sea. A sympathetic Neapolitan, Gonzalo, provided them with rich garments, linens, and other necessities. Gonzalo also provided Prospero with books from his library. Eventually, Prospero and Miranda arrived on the island, where they have remained since that time.

When he finishes the tale, Prospero uses his magic to put Miranda to sleep. The sprite, Ariel, appears as soon as Miranda is sleeping and reports on the storm, the ship, and the passengers. Ariel relates everyone, except the crew, was forced to abandon ship. Ariel tells Prospero that the passengers have been separated into smaller groups and are on different parts of the island; that the ship, with its sleeping crew, is safely hidden in the harbor; and that the remainder of the fleet, thinking that the king is drowned, has sailed home. Ariel then asks that Prospero free him, as had been promised. But Prospero has more need of his sprite and declares that Ariel's freedom must be delayed a few more days.

When Ariel leaves, Prospero awakens Miranda and beckons Caliban, the son of the witch, Sycorax. Caliban has been Prospero's slave, but he is insolent and rebellious and is only controlled through the use of magic. Caliban claims the island as his own and says that Prospero has tricked him in the past. Prospero is unmoved, claiming that Caliban is corrupt, having tried to rape Miranda. Prospero threatens and cajoles Caliban's obedience, but Caliban's presence makes Miranda uneasy.

After Caliban leaves, Ariel enters with Ferdinand, who sees Miranda, and the two fall instantly in love. Although this is what Prospero intended to have happen, he does not want it to appear too easy for Ferdinand, and so he accuses Ferdinand of being a spy. When Prospero uses magic to control Ferdinand, Miranda begs him to stop.

Commentary

Prospero tells Miranda their history as a way to inform the audience of this important information. In addition, the audience needs to know what events motivate Prospero's decision to stir up the storm and why the men onboard the ship are his enemies—several share responsibility for Prospero's isolation. By sharing this information, Miranda—and the audience—can conclude that Prospero is justified in seeking retribution. At the very least, Prospero must make Miranda sympathetic to this choice. It is also important that Prospero gain the audience's sympathy because his early treatment of both Ariel and Caliban depict him in a less than sympathetic light.

Character Insight

Ariel and Caliban are both little more than slaves to Prospero's wishes, and, in the initial interactions between Prospero and Ariel and Prospero and Caliban, the audience may think Prospero callous and cruel. He has clearly promised Ariel freedom and then denied it, and he treats Caliban as little more than an animal. The audience needs to understand that cruel circumstance and the machinations of men have turned Prospero into a different man than he might otherwise have been. But Prospero's character is more complex than this scene reveals, and the relationship between these characters more intricate also.

During the course of the story, Prospero repeatedly asks Miranda if she is listening. This questioning may reveal her distraction as she worries about the well-being of the ship's passengers. Miranda is loving toward her father, but at the same time, she does not lose sight of the human lives he is placing at risk. However, his questioning is equally directed toward the audience. Prospero also wants to make sure that the audience is listening to his story, since he will return to the audience in the Epilogue and seek their judgment.

It is clear from Prospero's story that he had been a poor ruler, more interested in his books than in his responsibilities. Prospero, therefore, is not entirely blameless in the events that occurred in Milan. Antonio could not so easily seize power from an involved and attentive ruler. This information mitigates Antonio's actions in seizing his brother's place and is important because this play is not a tragedy. In order for the comedic or romantic ending to succeed, none of the villains can be beyond redemption or reconciliation. It is equally important that Prospero not be beyond redemption. Prospero must be heroic, and this he cannot be if he is perceived as vengeful. Ariel reassures the audience (as well as Prospero) that the ship and its crew have been saved and the passengers are safely on the island. No one has been hurt or lost at sea.

Character Insight

In addition to relating the past, this act also helps define the main characters and anticipate the future. Prospero has been injured, and he intends to serve justice on his captives. He delves in magic and has developed powers beyond those of his enemies. He is also intelligent enough and strong enough to control the spirits on the island; for example, he can control Caliban, who is not without power of his own. Prospero uses the magic of nature, a white, beneficent magic that does no harm. He does not use the black magic of evil. Prospero has learned of this magic, not through the use of witches or evil spells (as did the witches in *Macbeth*), but through his studies. Prospero's white magic has supplanted the black, evil magic of Caliban's mother, Sycorax, because Prospero, himself, is good.

Any initial concern that the audience might have because of Caliban's enslavement evaporates at the news that he attempted to rape Miranda. His subsequent behavior will further prove his character, but he can be redeemed, and his redemption is necessary if the play is to succeed. Furthermore, Caliban, who is initially bad and represents the black magic of his mother, serves as a contrast to the goodness of Ferdinand and Miranda. The young lover's are instantly attracted to one another, each one a mirror image of the other's goodness. It is their goodness that facilitates the reconciliation between Prospero and his enemies. In this reconciliation lies Ariel's freedom and Caliban's redemption.

Glossary

betid   happened or befell; here, it means that nothing has happened to the boat's inhabitants.

teen   injury or harm. Prospero worries about the trouble that he has created for Miranda.

Signories   domains or city-states in Northern Italy, subject to the rule of a lord or signior.

inveterate   firmly established over a long period.

extirpate   to pull up by the roots. The reference here is to Prospero and Miranda's being forced from their home and country.

bark   any boat, but especially a small sailing ship.

trident   a three-pronged spear used by a gladiator in ancient Roman gladiatorial combats and by the Greek god of the sea, Neptune.

Bermoothes   refer to the Bermudas, a common word to describe tempests and enchantments.

twain   two. Ferdinand refers to himself and his father as but two of the victims of the storm.

surety   a person who takes responsibility for another. Miranda will be Ferdinand's guarantee.

Act II
Scene 1

Summary

This scene opens with all the passengers from the ship, except for Ferdinand, gathered on stage. Gonzalo begins with a speech celebrating their survival of the storm and their relative safety on the island, but King Alonso cannot be cheered because he is sure that his missing son, Ferdinand, has drowned. In the meantime, Antonio and Sebastian whisper among themselves and belittle both Alonso's grief and Gonzalo's cheer.

When Antonio and Sebastian join the general conversation around the king, they make no attempt to soothe him. Instead, they tell Alonso that he should not have permitted his daughter to marry the African. Sebastian tells Alonso that, had he not permitted the marriage, the royal party would not have been at sea and, thus, never in the storm. In short, Ferdinand would still be alive if Alonso had acted properly. These are harsh words to the grieving father, and Gonzalo gently chastises Sebastian for his insensitivity.

Ariel now enters, unseen by the group on stage, and puts all of them to sleep, except for Sebastian and Antonio. Left awake, Antonio and Sebastian devise a plot in which Sebastian will seize his brother's crown, much as Antonio had years earlier seized his brother's title and property. Although Sebastian has some concerns of conscience, Antonio dismisses such worries and urges action while everyone is asleep. Sebastian needs little convincing, and with Antonio, the two draw their swords and advance on the sleeping king and his party.

At this moment, Ariel takes action. He awakens Gonzalo in time to prevent the murders. Antonio and Sebastian quickly concoct a story to explain their drawn swords, warning of great noise, as if from bulls or lions. Alonso is easily convinced of his brother's sincerity, and the scene ends with the royal party leaving the stage in search of Ferdinand.

Commentary

This act better defines the personalities of the king's party and more clearly establishes the good characters from the bad. Alonso's first thought is for his son's well-being. In Act I, Prospero's tale of Alonso's complicity in his personal tragedy created an image of an uncaring ruler, one who was willing to overlook Antonio's deceit as long as it was beneficial to the king. But now, the picture is that of a grief-stricken father, beyond comfort. Alonso says little, but Gonzalo's efforts to care for and cheer his king, and the efforts of Adrian and Francisco to comfort their king, reflect well on Alonso's character.

Gonzalo's character is also realized in more depth than in Act I, where his attention was focused on the storm and on the boatswain's insolence. Beyond the efforts to comfort and reassure his king, Gonzalo relates a vision of a utopian society. In this society, he would be king. There would be no commerce or law and no servant class. No one would grow food, and no one would work. Nature would simply create all that men needed. This vision reveals that Gonzalo, too, has some concerns about authority and privilege. In Gonzalo's vision, there would be no inherited wealth, and land would not be enclosed. Thus, there would be no aristocracy and no country estates. In short, the source of many of the conflicts that exist in English society would be eliminated. Gonzalo wants the authority that Alonso holds, since Gonzalo would be king in this visionary world, but he lacks the impetus to put his dreams into actions, as Antonio and Sebastian would do. In spite of his dreams of personal grandeur, Gonzalo is capable of seeing the positive aspects of their situation. He alone realizes that their survival of the storm is an achievement. He is thankful that they have landed on such a lovely island, and he remains hopeful that Ferdinand has survived. Gonzalo's outlook is positive in many ways, but his utopian dream indicates that there is a complexity to his personality. On the surface he appears happy with his situation, but his dreams of being king reveal that he is not completely satisfied with his lot in life.

In contrast, Antonio and Sebastian's characters are developing as unpleasant and arrogant. Their sarcastic asides counter Gonzalo's good humor. They justly point out the flaws in Gonzalo's utopian dream, but they go beyond pointing out the flaws to compete between themselves to see who can devise the cruelest ridicule of both Alonso and

Gonzalo. The two are reminiscent of schoolboys, who giggle and whisper in the back of a classroom, in defiance of their teacher. And like schoolboys, Antonio and Sebastian are capable of cruelty, as when they tell Alonso that had he not married his daughter to the African, they would not be on this journey and Ferdinand would not be drowned. They are more than thoughtless and cruel, since they are also capable of forming a conspiracy to murder their king and Sebastian's brother.

Theme

Sebastian and Antonio's action hearkens back to the scene between the boatswain and Alonso in Act I. Alonso is king and represents authority. To plot his murder and to seize the crown is to usurp authority given by God. In England, the idea that a king was anointed by god was a crucial point in maintaining authority over the people. To kill God's representative on earth was a rebellion again the highest authority in the heavens. These two conspirators seek greater freedom and power than they are entitled to, and so they plot a coup. However, they forget that they are stranded on this island, with no kingdom to assume. Their plot to make Sebastian king neglects to ask king of what? They are far from Naples, with little expectation of rescue. Indeed, they never mention rescue, and thus, their plot to murder the king and seize his title would make Sebastian king of nothing.

The blending of illusion and reality, which was created in Act I with the imaginary storm, is carried forward in this scene, with Gonzalo's observation that their clothing is unharmed by the salt water, appearing as it did before the storm occurred. Gonzalo envisions a utopia, but the impossibility of such a thing happening is best illustrated by Antonio and Sebastian's plot. Even when there is no reason to plot a murder, they do so. It is in their nature, and one reason why Gonzalo's vision lacks reality is simply because it neglects to consider human nature, which fails to bow to illusion.

The party's whole existence on the island is an illusion and nothing is as it appears. Behind the scene and watching and manipulating all the action is Prospero. Although he never appears in this scene, he is very much present, functioning as a god-like entity. Antonio and Sebastian's swords are stayed because a higher authority prevents their actions. Prospero functions as a god would, protecting the innocent and guiding the action. However, Prospero is not a god, and that, perhaps, is the greatest illusion of all.

Glossary

tawny brownish-yellow; here used to mean that the sun has turned the ground a parched brown color.

rate opinion.

bourn a limit; boundary. Here used to mean that no land would be divided among landowners.

foison plenty; here, specifically, an abundance of produce.

hereditary sloth the natural inclination of a younger brother to be lazy, according to Sebastian, who sees the lack of a hereditary title as a reason to achieve nothing on his own.

feater more graceful. Here, Antonio's new rank—and clothes that befit it—looks graceful on him.

kibe a chapped or ulcerated sore, esp. on the heel. If Antonio's conscience were a sore on his foot, Antonio might put on a slipper.

Act II
Scene 2

Summary

The scene opens with Caliban cursing Prospero. When he hears someone approach, Caliban assumes it is one of Prospero's spirits, coming to torture him once again. Caliban falls to the ground and pulls his cloak over his body, leaving only his feet protruding. But instead of Prospero, the king's jester, Trinculo, enters. Trinculo is looking for shelter from the coming storm when he sees Caliban. With his body partially covered with the cloak, Caliban appears to be half man and half fish, or at least that is Trinculo's initial impression. Trinculo immediately sees the possibilities that this find presents. He can take this "monster" back to civilization and display it, charging admission to spectators who want to view this aberration of nature. Yet after touching Caliban, Trinculo decides that his "find" is not half man–half fish, but an islander. With the coming storm, Trinculo decides to seek shelter under Caliban's cloak.

The king's butler, Stefano, enters, clearly drunk. Stefano stops at the sight of the object on the ground, covered with a cloak and with four legs sticking out. Like Trinculo, Stefano immediately sees the financial possibilities that such a creature offers back home. But all of Stefano's poking has alarmed Caliban, who thinks that he is about to experience a new form of torture, beyond what Prospero has provided.

After pulling the cloak from Caliban's head, Stefano begins to pour wine into Caliban's mouth. Trinculo emerges from under the cloak and, happy to find another survivor of the storm on the island, joins Stefano and Caliban in drinking wine.

Caliban drunkenly watches the happy reunion of Stefano and Trinculo and decides that Stefano is a god, dropped from heaven. Caliban swears devotion to this new "god," and the three leave together, amid Caliban's promises to find Stefano the best food on the island.

Commentary

For the first time, the audience is given a close look at Caliban, who appeared only briefly in Act I. He appears now, cursing Prospero, and so, the depth of Caliban's animosity is quickly evident. He is very frightened by Prospero, whom he both cowers before and hates. Prospero has made Caliban his slave. The island was originally Caliban's, and he lived under no man's control.

Although Caliban blames Prospero for all his troubles, it is clear that nature, itself, has turned against him. In his soliloquy that opens this scene, Caliban admits that the animals on the island make faces at him, bite him, and hiss at him. This he blames on Prospero, reasoning that he controls all nature. Every noise is thought to be a spirit, sent by Prospero to torture him. Caliban represents nature, unfettered by man's domesticity—nature, as it appears untouched by corrupt forces. And yet Caliban is not totally innocent. Prospero has already told the audience of Caliban's attack on Miranda. His behavior recalls the undisciplined nature of wild animals rather than that of natural man. He has not been civilized to the rules of social discourse and, instead, functions as the animals in the forest do—obeying the instincts of nature.

If Caliban represents the most basic elements of nature, then Stefano and Trinculo represent how low civilized men can sink without self-control. Both men are opportunists, ready to exploit the new "man" they discover under a cloak. Both Stefano and Trinculo share the same initial thought—how to make money from a being as unusual in appearance as Caliban. They immediately see the potential in exhibiting him as a freak of nature.

Of course, Shakespeare is commenting on a real phenomena in English society: the exhibition of American Indians, transported back to England from the new colonies in Virginia. Elizabethan entrepreneurs quickly saw a profit in the "natural" people who inhabited the Americas. These Native Americans were brought to England and displayed for profit. Most quickly succumbed to diseases for which they had no natural immunity. But more of these natural people were readily available, and so the trade continued for some time. Stefano and Trinculo's thinking reveals them to be little more than charlatans, out to make a quick profit.

Stefano and Trinculo readily fall into agreement with Caliban and plot to commit murder because they think there is a profit to be made.

But there is another reason, as well. Stefano enjoys his new status as Caliban's god. He delights in the adoration, the reversal of fortune. He has gone from butler to god and sees it as a huge improvement in status. Just as Sebastian and Antonio expect power as a reward for violent behavior, the butler and the court jester would like power with a minimal amount of effort. If murdering Prospero will make them kings of the island, they are ready to do Caliban's bidding. Of course, just as Sebastian and Antonio were being watched, so too are these three drunken conspirators.

Style & Language

This scene involves low comedy, the kind of slapstick that depends more on actions than words. Caliban, Stefano, and Trinculo are funny because the audience thinks their efforts ridiculous. Trinculo is dressed as a clown, and Trinculo rode the storm to safety in a wine cask. Although Sebastian and Antonio's plot might represent real danger to Alonso (if Prospero were to permit it), Trinculo and Stefano's plot can only represent impotence. Their plan to murder Prospero and ravish Miranda is doomed from the start, and the audience is always aware of this. In their drunkenness, they are ineffectual and thus can be enjoyed. In Caliban's innocence, he has allied himself with buffoons. He bribes his accomplices with promises of choice foods and is too unsophisticated to realize that these men would also enslave him if given the opportunity. Stefano and Trinculo represent the worst that civilization has to offer—debauchery and absurdity.

Glossary

inch-meal   inch by inch. Here, Caliban hopes for Prospero's fall.

bombard   a large leather container meant to hold liquor.

swabber   the sailor who washes the ship and keeps the decks clean.

chaps   jaws. Stefano is telling Caliban to open his jaws and drink more.

long spoon   alluding to an old proverb that a man must have a very long spoon to eat with the devil. Stefano thinks that Trinculo is a ghost.

moon-calf   [Obs.] a monstrosity; a misshapen creature born under the moon's influence.

Scamels   The meaning is uncertain but thought to be either shellfish or rock-inhabiting birds.

Act III
Scene 1

Summary

Ferdinand enters carrying a log, which he claims would be an odious task except that he carries it to serve Miranda. His carrying of the logs is a punishment but one he willingly accepts because thoughts of Miranda make the work seem effortless.

Miranda enters and, when Ferdinand will not rest, offers to take up his chore so that she might force him to rest, but Ferdinand refuses. Although she was instructed not to reveal her name, Miranda impulsively divulges it to Ferdinand. Ferdinand, for his part, has known other beautiful women, but he admits to having never known one as perfect as Miranda. Miranda confesses that she has known no other women, nor any other man, except for her father. Now, she would want no other man except for Ferdinand. At this, Miranda remembers that she has been instructed not to speak to their guest and momentarily falls silent. When Ferdinand avows that he would gladly serve her, Miranda asks if he loves her. At his affirmative reply, Miranda begins to weep. She tells Ferdinand that she is unworthy of him but will marry him if he wants her. He quickly agrees, and the couple finally touch, taking each other's hands, as they pledge their love.

Prospero has been listening, unseen. He acknowledges Miranda and Ferdinand's natural match as being "Of two most rare affections" (75), but he has other plans that need his immediate attention, and so he turns to his books and other waiting business.

Commentary

This scene leaves no doubt that Prospero is the absolute ruler of his small island. Ferdinand is set to the same task as Caliban, carrying logs. Although he is a prince, Ferdinand must bow to the same authority that Caliban, a slave, observes. Even Miranda is not exempt from Prospero's rule. She is not supposed to speak to Ferdinand. Moreover, she is not permitted to even give him her name, although she does. As part of

Prospero's power, he must pretend to oppose the romance between Miranda and Ferdinand; however, the audience knows that Prospero is not opposed to such a union, and in fact, he had hoped that they would love one another. But Prospero must maintain the illusion that he is in absolute control, and so, he imposes rules to guarantee his authority.

In part, Prospero is playing the role that any father must play when his daughter has a suitor. Protecting Miranda's worth is tied to protecting her virginity; thus, he watches the courtship, unseen. Miranda is an obedient daughter, as proved by her dismay when she forgets herself and reveals her name to Ferdinand. But she is also a young woman in love, and when her father is occupied, she immediately looks to release Ferdinand from his labors.

Miranda has no experience with people. She has never seen another woman and does not know that she is beautiful. She has no experience with men, other than her father and Caliban. Because of her isolation, she has developed no artful skills at flirting, and when Ferdinand tells her that he loves her, Miranda weeps. Their love scene is sweet and tender, and without artifice. Prospero watches this exchange, not just to control its outcome, but to protect his only child. Miranda is more vulnerable than most young women, and she needs a strong father to protect her. As such a strong authority figure, Prospero is well suited to protect Miranda from any dangers that this new experience might present. But his watchful observances also recall the godlike control that he has exercised over every other individual being and every action that has occurred on the island.

Literary Device

This loving scene serves as a bridge between two scenes of low comedy. Wedged just before and just after, this romantic interlude reminds Shakespeare's audience of the contrast between the pure and tender love of Ferdinand and Miranda and the debauchery of Caliban, Stefano, and Trinculo. Ferdinand's labors are willingly accepted, because Miranda's mere presence fills all his work with pleasure. This happy labor contrasts to the cursing that opened the previous scene, when Caliban also carried logs. Ferdinand and Miranda's love embodies an ideal love, one in keeping with the expectations of nature. There is gentle humor and genuine heartfelt feelings, and there are none of the artificial trappings of conventional courtship.

Character Insight

Both Ferdinand and Miranda express their feelings honestly and with dignity. Their encounter adds something important that had been missing—authentic nobility of manner. Their nature, or breeding, has led them to behave with deportment, as would be expected of the children of the aristocracy. Both young lovers behave in a responsible manner that was missing from their fathers' lives. Thus, Ferdinand and Miranda fulfill the promise of reconciliation, which is an important element of this play. The plotting and betrayal of the fathers is atoned for by their children. For this to work successfully, Alonso and Prospero's children must be elevated far above their fathers in both decorum and honor.

Glossary

hest   [Archaic] a behest; a bidding; an order. Miranda was commanded not to reveal her name.

foil   to keep from being successful; thwart; frustrate.

wooden slavery   being compelled to carry wood.

hollowly   here, insincerely.

maid   here, handmaiden, a woman or girl servant or attendant.

Act III
Scene 2

Summary

This scene returns to Stefano, Trinculo, and Caliban—all of whom are now very drunk. Caliban has a plan to kill Prospero and elicits help from his new friends. As Caliban explains that he is the rightful owner of the island, Ariel arrives and listens attentively. Caliban explains that they must burn Prospero's books, and after Prospero is dead, Stefano can marry Miranda, which will make her his queen of the island. Trinculo agrees to the plot.

Ariel resolves to tell Prospero of the plot against him. When the drunken men begin singing, Ariel accompanies them on a tabor and pipe. The men hear the music and are afraid, but Caliban reassures them that such sounds are frequently heard on the island. Stefano finds the idea of free music a strong promise of his success on the island, and three drunken conspirators follow the sounds of the music offstage.

Commentary

Caliban represents untamed nature in conflict with civilization. He intuitively understands that Prospero's power comes from his books; thus the books are to become the first victims of his rebellion. Prospero's books represent oppression to Caliban because all that Prospero's civilization and books have to offer is slavery. Although Caliban might be considered an uneducated savage by Elizabethan accounts (and perhaps by modern accounts, as well), he existed quite happily on the island before Prospero's arrival. Civilization transformed Caliban from freedom to slavery, and he has received little benefit from Prospero's tutelage; even Caliban's use of language is limited to little more than cursing. Because civilization has failed Caliban, he quickly turns to the first possible source of help to appear: Stefano and Trinculo, the lowest forms of civilized behavior.

Caliban's island paradise is not all that different from Gonzalo's ideal natural world. Both Caliban and Gonzalo see their ideal worlds as untouched by the confinements of civilization. In both visions, nature provides whatever is needed, and mankind has little effect on the island's existence. But there is one substantial difference. Where Gonzalo would make himself king, Caliban dreams of living in peaceful isolation, with no king to abuse him. Yet, to secure his freedom from Prospero, Caliban would subordinate himself to Stefano, who would take Prospero's place as ruler.

Caliban is unable to appreciate that the crass butler, whom he has elevated to a god, would be a worse god than Prospero has been. After all, upon first finding Caliban, Stefano pulled Caliban's head back, forced open his mouth, and poured wine down his throat. His exploitation of Caliban, including the plan to exhibit him as a money-making proposition, reflects little concern for Caliban's well-being. Although Prospero's enslavement of Caliban also raises questions of propriety, his stated reasons are to restore order to the island. However, Prospero's sense of order ignores Caliban's needs. Caliban does not need civilization and its artifacts, education, and language to satisfy his needs. So desperate is Caliban to escape Prospero's oppression, that he would effectively trade one god for another: Prospero for Stefano. But Caliban appears unable or unwilling to comprehend this component of his plot. The murder of Prospero is his immediate concern, and he gives little thought to what might follow.

Caliban's plot to murder Prospero offers a parallel to Antonio's plot to murder Alonso. Caliban enlists the assistance of Stefano and Trinculo, just as Antonio enlists the support of Sebastian. Each group of conspirators ignores reason and logic. At the moment, they are all isolated on the island, with little hope or expectation of rescue. Alonso's murder will render no gain for Antonio or Sebastian, since Sebastian would be king of nothing. In a parody of Antonio's plot, Prospero's murder will provide little benefit for Caliban, except to trade one ruler for another and, perhaps, slavery for worse abuse. But both plots illustrate the potential for violence that exists in all levels of society, whether in the aristocracy of Naples or in the natural beauty of an isolated island.

Caliban, himself, is filled with contradictions. On one hand, he is brutal, instructing Stefano to "Bite him [Trinculo] to death" (32). Caliban also describes in detail his plans to murder Prospero by "knock[ing] a nail into his head" (59). Later, Caliban gives his co-conspirators many choices of ways to murder Prospero, from striking him on the head to disemboweling him to cutting his throat. Any means is acceptable, and, as a reward, Caliban casually promises them Miranda. The brutality of Caliban's plan is countered with the poetry of his descriptions of the island:

> The isle is full of noises,
> Sounds, and sweet airs, that give delight and hurt not.
> Sometimes a thousand twangling instruments
> Will hum about mine ears, and sometimes voices
> That if I then had waked after long sleep
> Will make me sleep again; and then in dreaming
> The clouds methought would open and show riches
> Ready to drop upon me, that when I waked
> I cried to dream again.

The songs that Caliban describes and the beauty of his dreams reveal a humanity that is lacking in his descriptions of the murder plot. Caliban is more than a wild beast of the island, and his personality is more complex than his brief scenes have thus far disclosed. The plot to murder Prospero is Caliban's rejection of civilization. He finds no alternative to brutality, if it will free him of the oppression of civilization. The natural beauty of the island permeates Caliban's world, but he is able to separate this beauty from the violent acts that he plans. In Caliban's world, there is no incongruity in the existence of both poetry and barbarity.

Glossary

case   here, prepared.

pied ninny   a fool.

patch   [Archaic] a court jester; any clown or fool.

murrain   a disease of cattle.

wezand   windpipe.

troll the catch   to sing the round lustily or in a full, rolling voice.

Act III
Scene 3

Summary

The royal party has searched futilely for Ferdinand and collapses, exhausted upon the beach. Unknown to the royal party, Prospero arrives and watches their actions. Within a few moments, a number of ghostly shapes arrive and with them, a lavish banquet. After gesturing to the party that they should approach and eat, the spirit shapes depart. The royal party is incredulous, but they are also hungry and ready to eat. Yet Ariel appears, disguised as a harpy. He makes the banquet disappear and accuses Antonio, Sebastian, and Alonso of being the instruments of sin. Although the men draw their swords, they are frozen in place by magic and unable to lift up their arms. The king is shaken by what he has seen and heard, and he flees, as do Antonio and Sebastian. Worried that they might do themselves harm, Gonzalo sends Adrian and Francisco to watch them.

Commentary

This scene provides the climax of Prospero's plan and the denouement of Antonio's many plots. Antonio, Sebastian, and Alonso are powerless against Prospero's magic. Their plotting against him—and Antonio and Sebastian's subsequent plotting against Alonso—is ineffectual in the face of Prospero's greater power. This is the moment of revenge that Prospero has awaited for 12 long years, and he offers no clue what form the punishment will take. However, because he has encouraged Miranda and Ferdinand's love, it is clear that any retribution directed toward Alonso will not be severe, since he would not risk his daughter's happiness in such a way. That is not the case, however, for Sebastian and Antonio, who have every reason for concern.

**Character
Insight**

As he has from the beginning, Ariel carries out Prospero's wishes efficiently and effectively. Ariel, who projects delicacy and eagerness in all that he does, is a spirit of the air. He is eager to be free, and his freedom has been promised in two days, at the conclusion of this mission. Ariel is eager to please Prospero, who freed him from Sycorax, the witch who had imprisoned him in a tree for refusing to do her bidding. Although he wants his freedom in exchange, Ariel approaches his tasks with enthusiasm, quickly doing what is asked and reporting promptly any activities that he observes. Earlier, Ariel had reported the plot to murder Prospero, and now he assists in punishing Prospero's enemies. Ariel's obedience is an important symbol of Prospero's humanity because he ameliorates Prospero's role on the island and humanizes the action that he takes against his old adversaries. Finally, Ariel's willing obedience of Prospero's wishes stands in stark contrast to Caliban's cursing and plotting against the same master.

This scene illustrates the deep disparity between what is real and what is imagined. The disappearing banquet was never real, although it briefly appears so to the hungry captives. Ariel appears briefly as a harpy, a mythical creature with a vulture's wings and claws and the face of a woman, yet it is not Ariel's voice that speaks but a deep voice that seems to come from the heavens. Neither the harpy nor the voice is real. None of this is real, and all of it is carefully staged, a theatrical spectacle designed to frighten and punish Prospero's enemies. Prospero is the puppet-master, carefully pulling the strings and manipulating the action. But he remains unseen and, like the deep voice and the banquet, even this scene is illusionary. His victims cannot know that Prospero waits, unseen in the wings. All that is real is the madness that this confrontation has evoked in the three sinners.

Glossary

Br'r lakin "By your ladykin"; a reference to the Virgin Mary.

a living drollery probably a puppet-show with live actors.

Wallets here, meaning wattle, the fleshy, wrinkled, often brightly colored piece of skin that hangs from throat of a turkey.

dowle small feather.

too massy unable to move. Here, through magic, the men are paralyzed.

bass my trespass Here, meaning that the condemnation (my trespass) was uttered in a deep bass voice. The thunder proclaimed his sin, according to Alonso, like a noise from the heavens.

Act IV
Scene 1

Summary

Prospero, acknowledging that he has been harsh, now promises a reward that will rectify the young lovers' momentary suffering. Recognizing Ferdinand and Miranda's love for one another—they have passed the trials that Prospero has set before them—he offers Miranda to Ferdinand as his wife. Prospero next calls Ariel to help stage a celebration of the betrothal. The celebration includes a masque, presented by the spirits of the island.

Suddenly Prospero remembers the three conspirators who have set out to murder him and calls a halt to the masque. He then summons Ariel, who reports that he led the three men, all of whom are very drunk, through a briar patch and into a filthy pond, where he left them wallowing. Prospero instructs Ariel to leave garish clothing on a tree to tempt the men.

Soon Caliban, Stefano, and Trinculo appear, foul smelling and wet. Stefano and Trinculo lament the loss of their bottles but are much cheered when they see the clothing hanging nearby. The two ignore Caliban's pleas to continue on their mission and his warnings that their hesitation will lead Prospero to catch them. At that moment, Prospero and Ariel enter with spirits, disguised as hunters and hounds. The three conspirators flee, with the spirits in pursuit. Prospero, acknowledging the power he now holds over all his enemies, promises Ariel that he shall soon be free.

Commentary

Within a few minutes of the opening of this scene, the betrothal is complete, and Miranda and Ferdinand's future has been determined to Prospero's satisfaction. The virtue and honor of these young people transcends the actions of their fathers and, in this betrothal, lies the redemption of their families. (According to Elizabethan custom, marriages consisted of three separate elements. The first was the betrothal, with it announcement of a promise to wed and the acknowledgement of the family's permission for the union to take place. The second part consisted of the wedding, with a religious ceremony that united the couple and bound them together under church law. The final part to the marriage was the consummation, the physical union of the couple through sexual intercourse.)

For the first time, Prospero can fully reveal his true nature. Finally, there is no need to be punitive or autocratic, and he can simply enjoy his daughter's happiness. For these few moments, the audience can witness what Prospero is like without the weight of revenge or control motivating his actions. Even in his gentleness and goodwill toward Ferdinand, Prospero does not forget that he is still Miranda's father, and as such, he is responsible for her until she is safely wed. Consequently, a significant amount of time is spent warning Ferdinand that he must control his lust until the wedding takes place. Prospero warns the young man that "barren hate, / Sour-eyed disdain, and discord," will be his reward if he cannot control his lust (IV.1, 19–20). All of this is in keeping with the expected parental role. Miranda is even more innocent than most young women, having had none of the socialization that other young women would experience. Because of her isolation, she is more vulnerable, and her father is aware of her purity of heart. However, he is also a father, facing the imminent loss of his only child, and so his excessive warnings to Ferdinand to control his lust are to be expected.

Literary Device

The betrothal ceremony is sealed with a masque, and, in keeping with the motif of reality and illusion, this masque draws on mythical goddesses and on Greek and Roman mythology. The goddesses are selected for their symbolism and connections to nature and represent the promise of fertility and fecundity, heavenly harmony, and an eternal springtime of love. As the goddess of the rainbow, Iris is the promise of spring rains leading to a bountiful harvest. As a messenger from Juno, she also represents the gods' blessing on this betrothal. When Juno appears, her presence affirms the blessing of the heavens, and since Juno is the goddess of marriage and childbirth, her presence is the promise of a happy union for the couple and a blessing of many children. Finally, Ceres' appearance also promises nature's blessing on this marriage. Together, the goddesses are the promise of celestial harmony, fruitful harvests, and eternal seasons without winter. Venus, with her emphasis on abandon and sexual love is deliberately excluded, since the focus of the masque is on honorable marriage.

The pastoral tradition focuses on a nostalgic image of the peace and simplicity of the life of shepherds and other rural folk in an idealized natural setting. Pastoral poetry is characterized by a state of contentment and a focus on the contemplative life. As is the case with most masques, Prospero's masque focuses on these pastoral motifs, with reapers and nymphs celebrating the fecundity of the land. The land is green, the harvesters sunburned, and the harvest worth celebrating. Love is innocent and romantic and not sexual. The country life, with its abundance of harvests and peaceful existence is an idealized world that ignores the realities of country life with its many hardships. But a wedding masque is not the time to remind the young couple of the possible hardships that they will face. Instead, Prospero focuses on the blessings of a happy marriage and the contentment that Ferdinand and Miranda will bring one another.

Theme

At the conclusion of the masque, Prospero addresses Ferdinand and tells him that "We are such stuff / As dreams are made on" (IV.1, 156–57). This is a reminder that the masque, with all its heavenly creatures, is not real. Like the masque, life, too, will come to its inevitable end. Prospero reminds Ferdinand that each man's life is framed by dreams. The evidence of that life, with its earthly possessions, is only temporary. Again, this points to the role of the young couple as redeemers for their father's sins. Alonso, and through him, Antonio and Sebastian, have placed too much emphasis on worldly possessions and titles. Even Prospero, with his focus on books, has forgotten that they are also only temporary vestiges in this life. This reminder that corporeal riches are only temporary also seems to be directed toward Stefano and Trinculo.

Many scholars and critics would like to see Shakespeare's autobiographical presence in Prospero's words. Those who think that Shakespeare is allowing Prospero to speak his farewell to the stage find "Our revels now are ended" to be a poignant reminder of the temporal plight of all men's lives. Since *The Tempest* comes near the end of Shakespeare's career and life, it is very tempting to read autobiography into Prospero's words. Still, his words may only be an impassioned reminder for each man to value life and accept its temporal limitations.

Character Insight

At the scene's end, Prospero must shrug off the mantle of fatherhood and assume the cloak of ruler and deal with the three conspirators who plot his death: Caliban, Stefano, and Trinculo. The punishment that Ariel reports is more nuisance than painful, another reminder that Prospero's retribution includes no serious injuries. Aside from a few scratches, the trip through the briar patch and the putrid pond only injure the men's pride. Even the spirit hunters and dogs that give Caliban, Stefano, and Trinculo chase are little more than air, not capable of causing their prey any harm. This mild punishment reflects Prospero's inherent good nature and his willingness to forgive his enemies. He will make them suffer for their plotting, but he will do them no real injury. Although it was not always clear earlier in the play, by this act, Prospero's true nature, his goodness and his humanity, have become clear to the audience.

Glossary

genius   either of two spirits, one good and one evil, supposed to influence one's destiny.

Phoebus' steeds   the mythological horses that drew the chariot of the sun. Here, the suggestion is that they are lame from the long day and overriding.

vanity   reference to an illusion or trick that Prospero has created.

abstemious   moderate, especially in eating and drinking; temperate. Prospero is warning Ferdinand once again about resisting lust before the wedding occurs.

bring a corollary   here, meaning to bring too many spirits rather than not enough.

amain   at or with great speed; here, Miranda's peacocks fly quickly.

sicklemen   reference to nymphs disguised as harvesters.

unbacked   not broken to the saddle: said of a horse.

trumpery   something showy but worthless; here, the gaudy clothing designated as bait for the three conspirators.

frippery   here, an old clothing shop.

dropsy   a disease characterized by the accumulation of fluid in the connective tissues, resulting in swelling.

jerkin   a short, close-fitting jacket, often sleeveless.

Act V
Scene 1

Summary

This scene opens with Ariel revealing to Prospero that Alonso, Sebastian, and Antonio are remorseful, worried, and desperate. Gonzalo is worried and grief-stricken at his king's pain. Prospero reassures Ariel that he will be compassionate in dealing with his enemies and asks that Ariel bring the group to him. While he is waiting for the king and his party to appear, Prospero soliloquizes about what he has accomplished with magic and, at the soliloquy's end, promises that he will now give up his magic, bury his magic staff, and drown his magic book at sea.

Almost immediately, Ariel enters with the royal party, who appear to be in a trance, and places them within the magic circle that Prospero had earlier drawn. With a few chanted words, the spell is removed. Prospero, clothed in the garments of the duke of Milan—his rightful position—appears before them. In a gesture of reconciliation, Prospero embraces Alonso, who is filled with remorse and immediately gives up Prospero's dukedom. Gonzalo is also embraced in turn, and then Prospero turns to Sebastian and Antonio. Prospero tells them that he will not charge them as traitors, at this time. Antonio is forgiven and required to renounce his claims on Prospero's dukedom.

While Alonso continues to mourn the loss of his son, Prospero relates that he too has lost his child, his daughter. But he means that he has lost her in marriage and pulls back a curtain to reveal Ferdinand and Miranda playing chess. Ferdinand explains to his father that he is betrothed to Miranda and that this event occurred while he thought his father dead. Alonso quickly welcomes Miranda and says he will be a second father to his son's affianced. At the sight of the couple, Gonzalo begins to cry and thanks God for having worked such a miracle.

Ariel enters with the master of the boat and boatswain. Although the ship lay in harbor and in perfect shape, the puzzled men cannot explain how any of this has occurred. Alonso is also mystified, but Prospero tells him not to trouble his mind with such concerns. Next,

Ariel leads in Caliban, Stefano, and Trinculo, who are still drunk. Prospero explains that these men have robbed him and plotted to murder him. Caliban immediately repents and promises to seek grace. The three conspirators, who have sobered somewhat since confronted with Prospero and the king, are sent to decorate Prospero's cell. Prospero invites his guests to spend the night with him, where he will tell them of his adventures and of his life during these past 12 years. Ariel's last duty to Prospero is to provide calm seas when they sail the next morning.

Commentary

Theme

This final scene indicates the extent of Prospero's forgiveness and provides an example of humanity toward one's enemies. Before he confronts his enemies, Prospero tells Ariel that "The rarer action is / In virtue than in vengeance" (27–28). That is, it is better to forgive than to hate one's enemies. This is the example that Prospero provides in reuniting everyone in this final scene. When he emerges from his trance, Alonso moves quickly to embrace Prospero, and just as quickly, he renounces his claims to Prospero's dukedom. This is the behavior the audience expects of Ferdinand's father, and it is what Prospero requires to resolve this conflict. Ferdinand is an honorable young man, filled with love and charity, and it is reasonable to expect that he learned these values from his father, even if his father has, on occasion, forgotten them. Alonso is honestly delighted in Ferdinand's engagement and welcomes Miranda with authentic grace. It is to be predicted that he is happy at recovering his son, but he is also clearly pleased to have gained a daughter. These spontaneous actions reveal that Alonso is as humane and honest as Prospero.

It is equally clear that Antonio and Sebastian each lack the humanity of their respective brothers. No apology is forthcoming from Antonio, and Sebastian thinks that Prospero is very likely the devil. Antonio never directly addresses Prospero, not even to justify his previous actions. And although both Prospero and Miranda might have died when cast out on to the sea some 12 years earlier, Antonio has no words for his niece. In spite of the obvious absence of regret from his brother, Prospero is true to his promise and seeks no revenge against Antonio. There is no reason to assume that shame restrains Antonio from speaking, and in all likelihood, he only regrets having been caught. Although Prospero warns his brother that he might still charge him with treason in the future, this warning is unlikely to restrain such a recalcitrant as Antonio.

Prospero's humanity is clearly obvious in his treatment of Antonio, whom he calls traitor but whom he declines to treat as a traitor. Critics and audience might be tempted to label Antonio as an unnatural brother, as would also be true for Sebastian. But their cruelty only indicates that nature provides for both goodness and evil. In the Christian world of the Shakespeare's time, evil is chosen, not destined, and nature provides for all outcomes, those who are virtuous and their counterparts, those who are corrupt. Hence, evil siblings are as natural as good siblings. Although the self-serving behavior of Antonio and Sebastian may be despicable, they are still a part of the natural world.

Character Insight

Caliban is also from the natural world, although as the child of a witch and devil. He is certainly different from the other humans on the island, but in this final scene, he displays more humanity than many of Prospero's "civilized" enemies. Antonio's only remark in this whole scene is to suggest that Caliban provides an opportunity to make money (V.1, 268–69). Antonio and Sebastian echo Stefano and Trinculo's earlier notion of exhibiting Caliban for profit, and in doing so, they reaffirm the impression that even the upper classes can be as lacking in morals as the two examples of the lower class, a butler and a court jester. Caliban, however, has risen above his companions and willingly admits his errors. In admitting his fault, Caliban proves himself more honorable than those who are socially his superior, Antonio and Sebastian.

Caliban is often celebrated as a natural man, one who is unspoiled by civilization. And yet, he easily embraces the worse that civilization has to offer. When exposed to Stefano and Trinculo, Caliban embraces their drunkenness and, in return, entices them to help plan a heinous crime. Many critics justify Caliban's actions by pointing to Prospero's persecution of Caliban. But nowhere in this play does Shakespeare validate this kind of revenge. Prospero may enslave Caliban, but he does not threaten his very existence. Certainly there is no way to justify slavery, and Shakespeare makes no attempt to do so. In the end, leaves Caliban to his island and to the natural world that he craves. The conclusion is about redemption, the personal redemption that so many of the participants reach. Caliban's regret during this final scene indicates he, too, has found the way to reconciliation.

Gonzalo is one of the few participants who has no need to ask forgiveness nor any cause to regret his actions. Upon discovering that Ferdinand is alive and that he is betrothed to Miranda, Gonzalo quite properly thanks God, who has "chalked forth the way" (206). Gonzalo also sees the irony in Miranda's offspring inheriting all that was her father's and all that belongs to his enemy. He also observes that there is much that has been restored: Ferdinand to his father, and with him, a wife. But there is more. Prospero's dukedom has been restored, as has the ship and all its missing crew. Yet more important than people or objects, other essential components of civilized society have been restored: authority, harmony, and order.

Even before this reconciliation scene occurs, Prospero has promised to put aside his magic and dispose of his magic book and staff, which are the source of his power. He has used magic to work in concert with nature, not to control or evoke evil. Now that he has his enemies under his control, Prospero permits compassion to replace magic. This putting away of his magic also signifies that Prospero's game is at an end. He has used magic to restore harmony and now needs it no more. The play ends with the promise of Ariel's freedom and the restoration of Prospero to a life filled with all that nature and God intended.

Glossary

mantle   to enclose or envelop.

furtherer   an accomplice.

rapier   a slender two-edged sword used chiefly in thrusting.

subtleties   here, the illusions.

requite   to make return or repayment to for a benefit, injury, and so on; reward.

tight and yare   sound and ready. The ship is ready to sail.

coragio   take courage (Italian).

Act V
Epilogue

Summary

Prospero, who is now alone on stage, requests that the audience free him. He states that he has thrown away his magic and pardoned those who have injured him. Now he requires that the audience release him from the island, which has been his prison so that he might return to Naples. The audience's applause will be the signal that he is freed. Prospero indicates that his forgiveness of his former enemies is what all men crave. With the audience's applause, Prospero leaves the stage.

Commentary

The Epilogue is often used to tie up loose ends and clarify any issues that remain unresolved. However, this epilogue does not provide the answers that the audience might expect. For instance, the audience never learns what is to become of Caliban or what will happen to Antonio and Sebastian. Few scholars ponder such questions. Instead, there has been a great deal of speculation on whether Prospero's farewell to magic is intended to announce Shakespeare's retirement from the stage. When Prospero asks the audience to free him from his imprisonment, is it instead the voice of Shakespeare asking the audience to free him from his craft?

Certainly, there are parallels between Prospero and Shakespeare to consider. Both are manipulators; Prospero manipulates everyone on the island, and Shakespeare manipulates the characters he creates and the plots he devises. Both create entertainment, Prospero the masque and Shakespeare his plays, and both are intent on retiring. It is easy to look at Prospero's words and imagine Shakespeare mouthing them as he retires from the stage. But such parallels do not necessarily reveal how the author was, could be, or wants to be. The words on the page, or now spoken before an audience, do not tell the author's intentions or tone. To attribute Prospero's words to Shakespeare's own life may be a fallacy. After the completion of Prospero's story, Shakespeare did continue to write, composing parts of three more plays. It would be unwise to focus solely on *The Tempest* as somehow representative of Shakespeare's farewell to the stage and thus overlook the many other important strengths of the play.

CHARACTER ANALYSES

Prospero

Prospero is the rightful duke of Milan. Twelve years earlier, he found refuge on this island after his younger brother, Antonio, seized Prospero's title and property. Prospero functions as a god on the island, manipulating everyone within his reach. He is helpless against his enemies until they appear on a ship nearby; but when they are close enough, he can use his magic to create a storm and bring them under his control.

Prospero's magic is the white magic of nature, not the black magic of evil men. This former duke of Milan is a complex personality. Although he refuses to free Ariel and enslaves Caliban, Prospero is really a beneficent ruler, never intending to injure even his enemies. Early in the play, Prospero appears callous and cruel, especially in his treatment of Ariel and Caliban. He is also autocratic in his treatment of Ferdinand, but Prospero realizes that Ferdinand and Miranda will value one another more if there are a few impediments to their courtship.

Prospero's humanity is clearly obvious in his treatment of Antonio, whom he calls traitor but whom he declines to treat as a traitor. Another example of Prospero's goodness is when he stops Alonso from apologizing to Miranda, telling him that there is no need for more amends. By the play's conclusion, it is clear that Prospero is just and fair, in addition to intelligent.

Ariel

Ariel is a spirit of the air who, because he refused to serve the witch, Sycorax, was imprisoned in a tree until rescued by Prospero. Ariel willingly carries out Prospero's wishes because he is eager to be free. Although he wants his freedom in exchange, Ariel approaches his tasks with enthusiasm, quickly doing what is asked and promptly reporting any activities that he observes. Early in the play, Ariel reports the plot to murder Prospero, and later, he assists in punishing Prospero's enemies. Ariel's obedience is an important symbol of Prospero's humanity, because he ameliorates Prospero's role on the island and humanizes the action that Prospero takes against his old adversaries. Finally, Ariel's willing obedience of Prospero's wishes stands in stark contrast to Caliban's cursing and plotting against the same master.

Caliban

Caliban is a product of nature, the offspring of the witch Sycorax and the devil. Prospero has made Caliban his servant or, more accurately, his slave. Throughout most of the play, Caliban is insolent and rebellious and is only controlled through the use of magic. Caliban claims the island as his own and maintains that Prospero has tricked him in the past.

Caliban represents the black magic of his mother and initially appears bad, especially when judged by conventional civilized standards. Because Prospero has conquered him, Caliban plots to murder Prospero in revenge. It is clear, though, that Caliban is a poor judge of character: He embraces Stefano as a god and trusts his two drunken conspirators to help him carry out a plot to murder Prospero. In many ways, Caliban is an innocent, reacting to emotional and physical needs without the ability to think through and fully understand the events and people who surround him. He is truly a child of nature, uneducated and reacting to his surroundings in much the same way that an animal does.

Miranda

Miranda is Prospero's daughter. She was 3 years old when she and her father were exiled. Now, some 12 years later, she is beginning to blossom into a beautiful young woman. She is an innocent, having never seen another woman and having no knowledge of any other human being, except for her father. She is unaware of her beauty because she does not know what feminine beauty is suppose to look like.

Miranda's compassion is evident in the first act, with her concern for the passengers caught up in the storm. Miranda is also justifiably indignant at her father's story of betrayal. Her tenderness is also evident when she begs her father not to use magic to control Ferdinand, whom she loves. Miranda is an obedient daughter, as proved by her dismay when she forgets herself and reveals her name to Ferdinand, but she is also a young woman in love, and when her father is occupied, she immediately looks to release Ferdinand from his labors.

Miranda has no experience with people, and she has no experience with men, other than her father and Caliban. Because of her isolation, she has developed no artful skills at flirting, and when Ferdinand tells her that he loves her, Miranda weeps. In all that she does, Miranda is sweet and pure, honest and loving.

Ferdinand

Ferdinand is the son of the king of Naples. During the storm, he is separated from the rest of the king's party. Once ashore, he meets Miranda and falls in love with her. Like Miranda, Ferdinand is honest and kind, a loving son, who will make a loving husband to Miranda. He easily reassures Prospero that he will respect Miranda's chastity and not violate the trust he has been given. Ferdinand also respects and loves his father. He makes a commitment to marry Miranda while thinking that his father is dead. When he finds that his father is alive, Ferdinand immediately acknowledges his father's authority and informs his father of his obligation to Miranda. Ferdinand is an honorable match for Miranda, sharing many of the same qualities that his innocent bride displays.

Alonso

Alonso is the king of Naples. When he believes that his son has died, Alonso is grief-stricken. Later, he is overjoyed to find Ferdinand still alive. Alonso bears some responsibility for the events in Prospero's life, because Antonio would not have acted without Alonso's agreement. However, when confronted with his responsibility, Alonso is genuinely repentant for the pain he caused Prospero in the past. Alonso's concern for his son's safety and his deep grief when he thinks his son is dead help to construct an image of Alonso as a good and loving father who has made mistakes in the past. The quickness with which he accepts Miranda as his daughter, as well as his attempts to apologize to her, also reinforce the image of Alonso as a good and just king.

Antonio

As Prospero's younger brother, Antonio is motivated by envy and by a desire to create trouble. He is now the fraudulent duke of Milan and is still actively engaged in plotting rebellion. His actions against Prospero were not sufficient to satisfy his ambitions, and now, Antonio convinces Sebastian to murder his brother. Although he may be frightened when confronted with the spirits and later Prospero, Antonio reveals no sign of remorse for the actions he has committed.

CRITICAL
ESSAYS

Caliban and the Natural World

As he did in many of his plays, Shakespeare uses *The Tempest* to ask questions about how well society and nature intersect. Most of the characters in this play exist in a civilized world, although certainly not all of them are civilized. Caliban, though, is referred to several times as a "natural man." What then does it mean in Elizabethan society to be a natural man, to exist as a natural man, as Caliban exists?

Caliban serves to illustrate ideas about the social hierarchy of the Renaissance world, which formulated a socially rigid—and very political—hierarchy of God, king, man, woman, beast. This order was based on the patriarchal tradition and the teachings of religious leaders, which postulate a hierarchical order for mankind based on physiological and physical characteristics. Other means of defining a place within this order were emotional stability and the ability to reason. Based on these definitions, beasts were lower in the evolutionary scale than all humans. According to this rather rigid social hierarchy, Caliban belongs at the bottom of the Elizabethan social hierarchy, having little perceived social worth. And yet, for many critics and students, he dominates *The Tempest*.

Caliban's Character

Prospero is really the center of the play, since the other characters relate to one another through him and because he manipulates everyone and everything that happens. The play ends with Prospero's victory over his enemies; he has the most lines, and he speaks the epilogue. Although he has far fewer lines than several other characters, Caliban, at only 100 lines, is often the focus of student interest, as well as that of many critics, often with an importance far greater than his actual presence in the play. Much of this interest reflects the social position of critics, scholars, and students. Whether Caliban is a monster, whether he is a victim of colonialism, or whether he represents some other disadvantaged element of society depends almost entirely on the social and cultural constructs and interests of the reader or audience. An important part of Caliban's appeal is his ambiguity of character.

The audience first learns of Caliban from Prospero's description to Ariel, in which the child of the witch, Sycorax, is described as "A freckled whelp, hag-born—not honoured with / A human shape" (I.2, 285–286). The audience learns more about Caliban's physical description from Trinculo and Stefano, who describe Caliban as less than human. Trinculo asks if the form before him is "a man or a fish?" (II.2, 24), and Stefano describes Caliban as a "moon-calf" (II.2, 104), a deformed creature. But it is not his appearance that makes Caliban monstrous in Prospero's eyes, nor was Caliban treated as a slave—at least not initially. Caliban, himself, relates that Prospero treated him well, teaching him about God when the two first met (I.2, 337–338). But it was Caliban's attack on Miranda that resulted in his enslavement and the change in Caliban's social position. Caliban sees the attempted rape of Miranda as a natural behavior. Had he not been stopped, Caliban would have "peopled else / This isle with Calibans" (I.2, 353–354). Reproductive urges are a natural function of animals, but humans modify their desires with reason and through social constraints. Without reason to modify his impulses, Caliban's behavior aligns him with the animals. Yet, at the same time, he is clearly more than a beast.

Critics make much of Caliban's name as an anagram for cannibal. However that does not mean that Shakespeare defines this character as someone who would eat people, as modern readers may assume. Instead, the Elizabethan meaning of cannibal is better described as someone who is a savage—uncultivated, uncivilized, untamed. Caliban is more closely defined as an innocent—more like a child who is innocent of the world and its code of behavior.

Many stage productions of *The Tempest* have depicted Caliban in varied ways—from the noble North American Indian, to African, to South American Indian or Mexican. But Shakespeare describes this creature as an innocent—perhaps half man and half fish. Trinculo and Stefano's descriptions are untrustworthy, since the first is frightened by the storm, and the second is drunk. What is clear is that Caliban's behavior suggests many questions about what is natural and what is unnatural. Is the attempted rape of Miranda or the plot to murder Prospero a natural behavior? These acts represent Caliban's attempts to survive, but this is not acceptable behavior among civilized men. These are the actions of wild, untutored animals. Caliban demonstrates no sense of morality nor any ability to understand or appreciate the needs of anyone other than himself. In Caliban's self-centeredness, he is little more than an animal. He wants to indulge his desires, without control. This is what being free means to Caliban, whose cry for freedom (II.2, 177–178) clarifies many of his actions.

Caliban's Relationship with Prospero

In Sir Philip Sidney's *Defence of Poetry* (1580), the author argues that poets have a responsibility to make learning more palatable through their art. Shakespeare fulfills Sidney's requirement by using his plays to explore complex ideas and issues, and thus, he makes learning more palatable for the audience. Prospero does the same thing when he uses his art to make Caliban's learning more palatable. Caliban is never harmed through Prospero's magic, and Prospero prevents Caliban from injuring anyone else. But Caliban does learn, through the use of Prospero's magic, that Trinculo and Stefano are not gods, nor are they honorable men who can be trusted. Trinculo and Stefano are really the dregs of society, useless opportunists, who think only of pleasure and greed. The ending of the play does not suggest their redemption. But the ending does suggest Caliban's. He is finally able to see Trinculo and Stefano for what they are, and he is able to reconcile with Prospero.

Rather than view the relationship between Prospero and Caliban as that of master and victim, consider instead that Prospero uses force to control Caliban not because he wants to dominate or enslave this natural man but because this is the traditional means to subdue a beast. Caliban's behavior is more closely aligned to the beast than to man, and thus, he must be controlled in a similar manner. By the play's conclusion, Prospero must forgive his enemies; this is, after all, a romantic comedy. But if Prospero is to fulfill Sidney's mandate, Caliban must also learn from his master how to be more human. His final speech (V.1, 298–301) indicates he has learned some valuable lessons.

Caliban's Humanity

Caliban is not the noble savage that is so often used to describe the victims of social injustice; instead he is the child of the witch Sycorax and the devil. So what is Shakespeare suggesting by making Caliban's parentage a byproduct of black magic and evil? *The Tempest* suggests that nature is more complex than it seems at first glance. The conclusion works to illustrate the best that human nature has to offer, through resolution and promise. Harmony and order are restored in a world where chaos has reigned—the natural world that Caliban covets. This natural world will be restored, but if the ending of the play is meant to suggest a restoration of order and a return to civilization, what then does the natural world represent?

Maybe this natural world is the world that a child of nature (like Caliban) needs, since he finds harmony there. But the natural world, with its own disorder, is not for everyone. Caliban's world is neither the ideal world nor the antithesis of the civilized world. It is only a different existence, one that Caliban is content to occupy. Perhaps Caliban continues to fascinate the audience and the reader because he is the Other, and there is no easy way to define him or to explain his purpose. Human nature is often brutal, sometimes evil, and perhaps we are meant to understand Caliban as being no better or worse than anyone who is wholly human.

Shakespeare was seemingly unconcerned about Caliban's humanity, or perhaps he just did not want to make understanding of humanity so easy for his audience. Either way, Caliban's meaning will no doubt continue to challenge the reader's preconceived ideas about what is monstrous, what is natural, and what is civilized in the world.

The Tempest as a Political Romance

Feminism was an important movement in seventeenth century England, generating many attempts by king, clergy, and male writers to suppress women's attempts to create a greater equality. Men's patriarchal concern about possible social changes was expressed in the many debates on this issue. Some of this concern was expressed in vehement sermons delivered by clergy and directed toward women, who were a captive audience forced to listen during church services.

Improvements in printing and less expensive books created an explosion of how-to pamphlets offering additional instruction for men on how best to control their wives and daughters. Patriarchy received additional support from both the Anglican Church and the Catholic Church, which advocated gender inequality as divinely ordained. According to the religious authorities of the period, women were inferior to men because the Bible says they are, or at least biblical scripture was interpreted in this way. The church blamed Eve, and through her all women, for man's fall from grace. Eve's story was interpreted to mean that all women needed to be suppressed and controlled. This control was especially important in a society in which women served as political currency. Women were the brides of kings and the mothers of future kings. Controlling their behavior and their sexuality was particularly important, thus the many references in *The Tempest* to Miranda's virginity.

Miranda is the only female character in *The Tempest*. On an island filled with men, her presence serves one important purpose—to provide a bride for Ferdinand, since by marrying him, she helps to bring reconciliation and redemption to their fathers, Prospero and Alonso. Miranda's primary value is in her virginity, which determines her worth on the marriage market. Upon seeing Miranda, Ferdinand quickly asks, "If you be maid or no?" (I.2, 431). His immediate concern is to her chastity. They love one another instantly, and if she is a virgin, she has value to Ferdinand, who can only wed a virgin. Virginity is a matter of politics. Ferdinand may love Miranda, but he cannot wed her unless she is pure. A man of property, especially a king or his son, must be assured that his offspring are truly his. A woman's virginity, which implies her chastity, is promise that her husband's paternity will never be questioned.

Miranda is a commodity, as was her mother, and her value as barter is in her nobility and purity. Virtue is a characteristic of nobility, and in telling his daughter about their past, Prospero emphasizes his own wife's nobility:

Thy mother was a piece of virtue, and
She said thou wast my daughter; and thy father
Was Duke of Milan, and his only heir
And princess no worse issued. (I.2, 56–59).

Prospero emphasizes that Miranda's mother was an excellent example of chastity and nobility, and her offspring is just as noble. Miranda is provided little information about her mother, except that which is most important about her—her chastity. The implication for Miranda is clear: Her value, too, is defined by her chastity. It is an interesting paradox that Miranda's sexuality serves as bait to entice Ferdinand, while at the same time, he is warned by Prospero not to touch the bait (IV.1, 14–23).

In fairy tales, the captive princess is usually rescued by the prince. In this case, Miranda and Ferdinand appear to rescue each other. He rescues her from isolation on the island and offers her both his love and a crown. She rescues him from her father, offering to help him carry logs and offering her love. However, the reality is that both young people are playing the role Prospero has mapped out for them. That Prospero loves his daughter is clear, but he also needs her to bring his plans to fruition. At the play's conclusion, Prospero's biggest success is in marrying Miranda to Ferdinand. Certainly, regaining his position as duke of Milan is important also, as is the redemption of Alonso. But both these events are tied to the marriage between Miranda and Ferdinand. These two young people represent the promise of the future, since this promised marriage ensures that Prospero's children will inherit from the king of Naples. Clearly, this union is a sizable victory for Prospero.

The 1613 presentation of *The Tempest* to celebrate Princess Elizabeth's coming wedding further reinforces the fairy tale elements, in which the princess is rescued by marriage, taken to a new land, and lives happily ever after. This was after all the plight of princesses everywhere, who were little more than political pawns in a game of diplomacy.

Political marriages—and the union of Miranda and Ferdinand is a political marriage—were normal parts of Elizabethan life. The audience learns in Act II that Alonso's daughter has been married to the king of Tunis. She was also married in opposition to her wishes, according to her uncle Sebastian, who reminds the king that Claribel (Alonso's daughter),

the fair herself
Weighed between loathness and obedience at
Which end o'th' beam should bow. (II.1, 129–131)

Claribel, although loath to marry her father's choice, had to weigh her obedience to her father against her own desires. Obviously, her obedience to her father weighed more heavily than her own desires about marriage. This supports the argument that a woman's primary value is as chattel, to be bartered on the marriage market for the husband her father most desires.

Politics is often a sleazy business. But that is not the case for Miranda, who has little awareness that she is a political pawn in Prospero's plan. Her sense that it is a "brave new world" (V.1, 186) reflects her innocence of both her role and of the life she will soon be leading, both as the wife of a king and later, perhaps, as the mother of a princess. Should Miranda eventually have a daughter, the daughter will also someday be bartered for a foothold in a kingdom or as an alliance to end a conflict. This was the expectation for daughters.

But not all women went willingly into the marriage market, and the new feminist movement seemed to offer support for revolt. Seventeenth-century drama was a safe way to explore the political and social issues of the period. Theater provided a voice and a way to disguise discussion of politically charged topics. If we examine *The Tempest* from this perspective, what is Shakespeare suggesting about the political use of women in contracting marriage? Shakespeare often used social issues as a way to explore the way society functioned, using the stage to present a microcosm that represented the larger macrocosm of the universe. The marriage relationship is a microcosm of the larger relationship between man and king, which was in turn a microcosm of the larger relationship between man and God. In focusing on the political implications of Miranda's marriage, Shakespeare is offering the audience a chance to consider the alliances that women form and the means by which they are constructed.

CliffsNotes Review

Use this CliffsNotes Review to test your understanding of the original text and reinforce what you've learned in this book. After you work through the review and essay questions, identify the quote section, and the fun and useful practice projects, you're well on your way to understanding a comprehensive and meaningful interpretation of The Tempest.

Q&A

1. Which definition do you think most accurately describes Prospero?

   a. self-centered, controlling, egotistical, disdainful

   b. godlike, manipulative, forgiving, loving

   c. godlike, controlling, arrogant, mean-spirited

2. Why is it necessary for Ferdinand to fall in love with Miranda?

   a. Ferdinand is under one of Prospero's magic spells and has no choice.

   b. Miranda is very beautiful and any man would love her.

   c. Their love is necessary to redeem the faults of their fathers.

3. When Stefano and Trinculo first see Caliban they immediate think that he is

   a. frightening and horrifyingly ugly.

   b. a good companion, who can help them find food.

   c. a way to make them rich, if they can get him back to civilized land.

4. Shakespeare uses the three unities of time, place, and action in this play, something he has only done in one other play (*The Comedy of Errors*). Why is it so important to make this play fit these unities?

   a. Shakespeare needed the unities to counter the incredulity of the magic and to add coherence to the plot.

   b. Shakespeare had only a brief time in which to present the play and did not want it to run longer than three hours.

   c. Shakespeare knew that Aristotle thought that the three unities were the most important features of a play, and this was Shakespeare's way of honoring Aristotle.

Answers: (1) b. (2) c. (3) c. (4) a.

Identify the Quote

1. They are both in either's powers. But this swift business
   I must uneasy make, lest too light winning
   Make the prize light.

2. The truth you speak doth lack some gentleness
   And time to speak it in. You rub the sore
   When you should bring the plaster.

3. We are such stuff
   As dreams are made on, and our little life
   Is rounded with a sleep.

4. The rarer action is
   In virtue than in vengeance.

Answers: (1) Prospero is the speaker in I.2, 454–456, explaining why he is making Ferdinand's wooing of Miranda difficult. (2) Gonzalo is the speaker in II.1, 136–138, chastising Sebastian for his lack of tact. (3) The speaker is Prospero in IV.1, 156–158, explaining to Ferdinand that each man's life is framed by dreams. (4) The speaker is Prospero in V.1, 27–28, stating his reasons for not harming his enemies.

Essay Questions

1. How does Prospero's magic differ from that of the witch, Sycorax?

2. Prospero's need for revenge could easily have led to tragedy. Compare *The Tempest* to one of Shakespeare's tragedies, such as *Hamlet*. What elements of revenge are present in both plays? How are they different? In what way is Prospero's revenge neutralized by romance?

3. Compare the plot to murder Prospero to the plot to murder Alonso. Shakespeare clearly intended one murder plot to mirror the other. What does each group of conspirators have in common? How important are social status and rank in evaluating these two murder plots?

4. Compare Gonzalo's ideas of the ideal society and commonwealth with those of Sir Thomas More in his *Utopia*. Why do you think that utopian dreams are destined to fail?

5. Traditionally, Shakespeare uses poetry for noble characters and prose for the lower class. Caliban, however, uses both poetry and prose. Discuss why he shifts between poetry and prose and under what circumstances. What does this reveal about this character?

Practice Projects

1. Shakespeare's plays are meant to be heard; thus, the plays are more easily understood if studied in performance. Selecting a seemingly difficult scene to present to an audience will add depth to your understanding of the text and make complex characters easier to grasp. For instance, Caliban's role is *The Tempest* is often misunderstood. Recruit two friends and together present Act III, Scene 2 to your classmates.

2. During Shakespeare's time, many people were opposed to the theater, arguing that

   a. Acting corrupts youth, by focusing on the unsavory elements of society: lascivious behavior and ungodly practices.

   b. Vagrants and thieves are drawn to the theatre, and as a result, crime increases.

   c. Servants and other working people neglect their work to go to the theatre, and this induces laziness.

   d. Crowds of people at the theatre lead to more illness, especially plague which spreads more easily in crowded public areas.

   e. Acting is lying, and so actors are dishonest people.

   Construct a chart that compares Elizabethan attitudes toward theatre with modern attitudes. On one side list the Elizabethan attitudes toward actors and the theatre, while on the other side, list the modern attitudes toward theatre or film. Be sure to include modern attitudes toward actors.

3. There are a number of paintings that illustrate *The Tempest* at the following Web site. After visiting this site, prepare an oral argument to present in class that explains the connections between theatre and art: www.cc.emory.edu/ENGLISH/classes/Shakespeare_Illustrated/TempestPaintings.html

CliffsNotes Resource Center

The learning doesn't need to stop here. CliffsNotes Resource Center shows you the best of the best—links to the best information in print and online about the author and/or related works. And don't think that this is all we've prepared for you; we've put all kinds of pertinent information at www.cliffsnotes.com. Look for all the terrific resources at your favorite bookstore or local library and on the Internet. When you're online, make your first stop www.cliffsnotes.com where you'll find more incredibly useful information about The Tempest.

Books

This CliffsNotes book provides a meaningful interpretation of Shakespeare's *The Tempest*. If you are looking for information about the author and/or related works, check out these other publications:

Shakespeare: The Invention of the Human, by Harold Bloom, focuses on Shakespeare's major plays. In this work, Bloom argues that much of what mankind thinks about humanity is derived from Shakespeare's plays. There are separate chapters on each of the plays. New York: Riverhead Books, 1998.

Shakespeare the Movie: Popularizing the Plays on Film, TV, and Video, edited by Lynda Boose and Richard Burt, is a collection of essays that explores the impact of the media on the study of Shakespeare. The essays contained in this collection examine the intersection of culture, literary criticism, and the literary canon. London: Routledge, 1997.

The Norton Shakespeare: Based on the Oxford Edition, edited by Stephen Greenblatt, et al, contains all the plays and poetry, arranged in chronological order. Each work is preceded by a careful discussion of the text, including sources and textual history. There is also extensive information about Shakespeare's life and the time in which he was writing. New York: W.W. Norton, 1997.

Women Reading Shakespeare, 1600–1900: An Anthology of Criticism, edited by Ann Thompson and Sasha Roberts, offers a comprehensive look at how Shakespeare has informed women's writing. Since Shakespeare's work first appeared, women have been writing in response to issues and ideas derived from the plays. Roberts includes many texts that are not generally available to readers, and thus, she provides a glimpse into the way early women writers were able to appropriate Shakespeare to meet their own needs. New York: St. Martin's Press, 1997.

Shakespeare in the Theatre: An Anthology of Criticism, compiled by Stanley Wells, is a collection of eyewitness accounts of the performances of Shakespeare's plays from the seventeenth century to the present. Many of the early reviews are not generally available, but these accounts of the plays reveals how the staging of the plays responded to the period and location of the production. London: Oxford University Press, 1997.

It's easy to find books published by IDG Books Worldwide, Inc. You'll find them in your favorite bookstores (on the Internet and at a store near you). We also have three Web sites that you can use to read about all the books we publish:

■ www.cliffsnotes.com

■ www.dummies.com

■ www.idgbooks.com

Internet

Check out these Web resources for more information about William Shakespeare and *The Tempest*:

Arden Net, www.ardenshakespeare.com/main/welcome.html—This site offers texts, resources, and general information about Shakespeare. This very useful site includes a review of Internet sites, a listing of professional organizations, essays on teaching, and lists of performances. Registration is free.

ELF Presents the Plays of William Shakespeare, www.theplays.org—This site includes texts of plays, characters guides, a glossary, and a chronology. Each play also includes a concordance, quotes, and a search engine.

Shakespeare's Globe, www.shakesperas-globe.org—This site includes information about the reconstruction of the Globe theatre in London. It includes a virtual tour and photographs. There is also information about performances and tickets and what to do when visiting.

Best Sites, daphne.palomar.edu/shakespeare/bestsites.htm—This site is considered to be among the best sites devoted to Shakespeare. It includes criticism, a biography, sources, and general historical information. There are also links to other sites.

Next time you're on the Internet, don't forget to drop by www.cliffs notes.com. We created an online Resource Center that you can use today, tomorrow, and beyond.

Films and Other Recordings

Following are some films based on *The Tempest:*

Forbidden Planet, MGM, 1956. This science fiction version of *The Tempest* is considered to be an entertaining film. Directed by Fred M. Wilcox.

The Tempest, Kino Video, 1979. This adaptation, filmed at Stoneleigh Abbey, focuses a lot on sex and nudity and uses only a little of the text. Directed by Fred M. Wilcox.

The Tempest, BBC Television, 1980. This is a British television production based on Shakespeare's text. Directed by John Gorrie.

The Tempest, Columbia, 1982. This film is a very loose adaptation of Shakespeare's play, in which a New York architect moves to a remote Greek island. Directed by Paul Mazursky.

The Tempest, The Bard Theatre/Kultur Video, 1983. The emphasis in this production is on magic and romance. Directed by William Woodman.

Prospero's Books, Video Treasures, 1999. This modern adaptation makes excellent use of special effects to focus on the magic in *The Tempest.* Directed by Peter Greenaway.

Journals

Check out these journals for more information on just about anything related to William Shakespeare:

The Shakespeare Newsletter is published four times a year. This useful newsletter provides information about Shakespeare Summer Festivals and performances of Shakespeare's works. The newsletter also contains articles that focus on plays and performances and recent Shakespearean criticism. Subscriptions are $12.00 per year. *The Shakespeare Newsletter* is published by the Department of English, Iona College, New Rochelle, NY, 10801. (914)633-2061, e-mail: SHNL@IONA.EDU.

Shakespeare Magazine is directed toward teachers and students but is of interest to anyone who loves Shakespeare. Typical issues contain interviews, photos, and discussion of upcoming productions and films, as well as articles of interest about Shakespeare's texts. Subscriptions are $12.00 per year. *Shakespeare*

Magazine is published by Georgetown University, P.O. Box 571006, Washington DC 20057-1006.

Shakespeare Quarterly is a scholarly journal, founded by the Shakespeare Association of America. This journal focuses on all aspects of Shakespearean study and includes essays and criticism. Subscription information, including cost, is available through the Folger Shakepeare Library. *Shakespeare Quarterly* is published by the Folger Shakespeare Library, 201 East Capital St., S.E., Washington, D.C. 20003-1094, (202)544-4600.

Send Us Your Favorite Tips

In your quest for knowledge, have you ever experienced that sublime moment when you figure out a trick that saves time or trouble? Perhaps you realized you were taking ten steps to accomplish something that could have taken two. Or you found a little-known workaround that achieved great results. If you've discovered a useful resource that gave you insight into or helped you understand *The Tempest* and you'd like to share it, the Cliffs Notes staff would love to hear from you. Go to our Web site at www.cliffsnotes.com and click the Talk to Us button. If we select your tip, we may publish it as part of CliffsNotes Daily, our exciting, free e-mail newsletter. To find out more or to subscribe to a newsletter, go to www.cliffsnotes.com on the Web.

Index

S